POSITIVE

MANAGEMENT

The new business agenda for the '90s focuses on working with change and developing people's potential and performance. The *People Skills for Professionals* series brings this empowering theme to life with a range of practical human resource guides for anyone who wants to get the best from their people in the world of the learning organisation.

Other Titles in the Series
COACHING FOR PERFORMANCE
A Practical Guide to Growing Your Own Skills
John Whitmore

CONSTRUCTIVE CONFLICT MANAGEMENT
Managing to Make a Difference
John Crawley

EMPOWERED!
A Practical Guide to Leadership in the Liberated Organisation
Rob Brown and Margaret Brown

LEADING YOUR TEAM
How to Involve and Inspire Teams
Andrew Leigh and Michael Maynard

MANAGING TRANSITIONS
Making the Most of Change
William Bridges

NLP AT WORK
The Difference that Makes a Difference in Business
Sue Knight

THE POWER OF INFLUENCE
Intensive Influencing Skills at Work
Tom Lambert

THE STRESS WORK BOOK
Eve Warren and Caroline Toll

POSITIVE MANAGEMENT

Assertiveness for managers

Paddy O'Brien

NICHOLAS BREALEY
PUBLISHING
LONDON

Dedication
to
Adrienne Boyle and Joan Orme:
both positive managers.

First published by
Nicholas Brealey Publishing Limited in 1992

21 Bloomsbury Way   Box 905
London   Sonoma
WC1A 2TH   California 95476

Reprinted 1994, 1995

ISBN 1-85788-008-0

British Library Cataloguing in Publication Data
A catalogue record for this book is available from the British
Library.

Printed in Finland by Werner Söderström Oy

Contents

Acknowledgements

I would like to thank all the friends and colleagues who have attended, discussed, refined, and developed assertiveness courses over the last few years: their shared creativity is at the heart of this book.

I am particularly indebted to Julia Pokora for her thinking on feedback and appraisals and Rod Lee for his comments on racism in corporate culture.

Colleagues who have lived and worked abroad helped me to form snapshots of how to pitch assertiveness in other cultures, and the insights in John Mole's book *Mind Your Manners* have also been invaluable.

Thanks to my editor, Nick Brealey, who has lived tolerantly with this book through all its incarnations.

Finally, my thanks and love to Tim.

Introduction 1

THE CHANGING MANAGEMENT ROLE

Managers have the dual role of reporting upwards to directors and implementing policy with staff. They often feel sandwiched between the two – sometimes blamed by both, almost always under pressure from both.

Rapid and radical economic swings have made the last decade particularly challenging both in industry and in the professions: the stress on management has increased accordingly because the necessary response to those swings has greatly changed the nature of many people's work. Being a manager in an enterprise which is highly geared and expanding is quite different from doing the same job in a company that has to streamline, re-think and rationalise. The job title might be the same but the job content is very different.

The international market continually throws up new circumstances to which managers must respond. It may happen through deliberate political change, such as the dropping of trade barriers throughout Europe, or through sudden international crises such as coups and wars.

The keynote is change. The successful manager is the one who survives and rides the changes. Riding changes well necessitates an ability to communicate clearly and well. It is the manager who has to communicate the directors' decisions to the staff, and the staff's reactions to the directors. She or he must explain changes, and control, motivate and get the best performance out of the staff. Assertiveness assists in all this. It will improve your ability in:

- negotiation
- being heard in meetings
- conflict resolution
- defusing anger
- communicating tough decisions
- implementing controversial policy
- standing your ground
- problem-solving
- explaining a process
- carrying out appraisals
- building a team

An ability to cope with all of these will become essential to managing well in the changeable 1990s.

ASSERTIVENESS IN MANAGEMENT

Assertiveness is sometimes thought of as the art of 'saying no'. This is because of its origins and growth within the women's movement in the 1970s and the importance it placed on being able to give clear refusals. While saying a good clear 'no' *is* an important assertive skill, assertiveness as a whole is about creative communication. It is concerned with the wider matter of positive or 'win–win solutions', i.e. solutions where both parties feel comfortable with and committed to the final plan.

Although assertiveness *is* about standing your ground when it is important to do so, it is also about balance and compromise. The strength derived from good assertive techniques may sometimes, significantly, be the strength to admit to a mistake or to leave an old and strongly held idea behind in order to develop a new one.

One Japanese commentator pinpointed the weakness of Western managers as their problem in finding a dignified and credible way of saying that they were wrong – 'they *always* have to say they are right'. Of course this blocks development, of both

the individual and the company. It is interesting to have this
behaviour identified, particularly by an observer from a culture
in which one can track spectacular industrial success to creative
communication between personnel.

Sir John Harvey-Jones observes an interesting aspect of
management in Japan:

> People think the Japanese are quick to take decisions. They're
> not in fact: they are extremely slow to take a decision, but
> once a decision is taken, everyone is so committed to it, and
> knows exactly what they have to do that they move at about
> three times the pace that we do. So they spend the time
> getting the commitment, and the commitment is got by
> masses of interaction.
>
> (Industrial Society pack on 'Leadership')

You cannot have 'masses of interaction' if one party in the
discussion feels that they have to 'say they are right' all the time.
Assertiveness can give the manager the confidence not to be
right sometimes in order to have 'masses of interaction'.

The change which this reflects is the acceptance of *yin* as well
as *yang* into management practice.

Historically, leadership skills have been based on the military
model: the ability to command firmly through a vertical
hierarchy. This emphasises 'masculine' energies and qualities,
the *yang* aspect of character and ability. The last two decades
have seen a growing value placed on 'feminine' or *yin* activities –
communication, cooperation and fusion – all these taking place
within flatter organisations. In their book, Peters and Waterman
tell us that:

> The models and metaphors of the past have been the
> manager as a cop, as a referee, as a devil's advocate, as a
> 'nay-sayer', as a pronouncer. The words we found that
> seemed much more appropriate in the excellent companies
> are the manager as a cheerleader, as a coach, as a facilitator,
> as a motivator of champions. The drum beat, and the down
> beat that has been so badly missing, was that it all comes
> from people.

Women and men can evolve a successful and powerful
management style by recognising and using both the *yin* and the
yang characteristics and behaviours in themselves. An inclusive
style like this requires self-awareness and poised interactive
behaviour. Of course it takes time to find out how this could

Yin/yang management

work for you, how you can find your personal yin/yang balance, the wavelength on which you are strong and positive but also flexible. The great advantage of learning assertiveness as a technique is that you have a practical framework within which to develop, a definite set of steps you can take in ordinary everyday life in the workplace.

Change is hard: habits of behaviour, habits in relationships, habits about self-regard and confidence (or lack of it) can set into patterns that feel inevitable. Assertiveness is a great help in 'scriptbusting' – breaking patterns you do not like, and developing more positive ones instead. All the relationships where you feel you pitched in far too aggressively and lost all hope of mutual trust, or far too friendlily and gave all your power away, *can* in fact be renegotiated.

Activities that drain the courage out of you – making presentations, managing disciplinary procedures, handling your own stress – can be reviewed and done differently if that is what you want. Because assertiveness helps you to avoid a passive attitude, it enables you to stand back and assess your current 'scripts' (habitual behaviours) without getting angry or overwhelmed by negative feelings about yourself.

Constructive change

Assertiveness also emphasises small achievable steps, and taking small achievable steps ensures that a process of change can go forward realistically and successfully. Managers who are used to analysing logistical problems in a step-by-step manner may not have thought of applying the same steady logic to their interpersonal dealings or their wish to improve intangible but vital matters, such as how they motivate their staff, or how they organise their time.

This balancing aspect of assertiveness is also there in its capacity for coping in a tough culture. If your working environment, or your market or your team challenge you and your personal power daily, you need great strength to survive and thrive. Here I think the calm power of assertiveness is analogous to the use of focused *ki* in the martial arts. Many senior martial arts gradings include a 'breaking' technique as part of the test – the candidate has to kick through a piece of wood, or a breeze block, or a brick, or make a knife hand strike through a stack of tiles. These tests are particularly pressurising because no practice is allowed; if you have learned your technique properly, it just works.

What one learns from taking part in this kind of test is that, once the technique is correctly learned, you accomplish the break with a *gentle* strength. If you hit a pile of tiles hard you just hurt your hand. If you hit it gently, with focused *ki*, your hand sails straight through. With assertiveness you can find ways of holding onto your personal power in threatening situations that do not require a lot of overt 'hard-hitting' strength. 'Hard-hitting' strength takes a toll on the person using it, just as striking the tiles hard hurts one's hand. Gentle focused strength and good technique get a much better result, enabling you to thrive in a tough culture without damage.

Although no one untrained in martial arts should try out knife hand strikes on roof tiles, managers can gain a great deal by learning and practising assertiveness methods in their professional lives.

Assertiveness is a style of clear and powerful communication based on analytical thinking and good self-respect.

It is a technique which can be learned in a step-by-step manner, and practised, alone or in group training sessions, and then used in 'real life'.

Although at first it may feel artificial, this technique quickly becomes an asset. Firstly, it provides a facility to assess situations logically, sort your possible responses calmly, pick the best, and communicate it clearly. Secondly, the methodical nature of assertiveness makes it possible to 'act over your feelings' – that is, to look confident even when you don't feel it, to appear calm even when you feel rattled, and to stand your ground even when you are under pressure. Thirdly, because active listening is as much at the heart of assertiveness as clear speaking, your people-management is much improved. Your staff feel: 'here is someone I can really talk to'.

Anyone can learn the technique and adapt it to suit their own particular job and their own individual temperament. It is a key skill for any manager as the 21st century approaches, enhancing the ability to negotiate, troubleshoot, train and present, to manage up *and* down the line.

Gentle strength is tough

HOW TO USE THIS BOOK

Part I of the book explains what assertiveness is (Chapter 2) and how to do it (Chapter 3). The Assertiveness Workshop in Chapter 4 is a step-by-step guide to development at work which can be done alone or with a partner, or adapted to fit staff training sessions. Readers can develop their own assertiveness skills by making their own selection of exercises as they go along. This will focus the reader's understanding of what assertiveness is and how it works. It can be applied in real-life situations as soon as you feel ready.

Part II of the book examines specific areas of managerial concern, and, illustrated with real examples, shows how assertiveness can improve management performance. The areas covered in detail include the whole range of behaviour and power-broking in meetings (Chapter 5), how to apply assertiveness methods in high-stress or high-emotion encounters where what the manager needs is that particular quality known as 'bottle' (Chapter 6). The important factors in motivation and leadership (Chapter 7), how to cope with both criticism and praise (Chapter 8), and how to take a lead in implementing equal opportunities and to meet the challenge of dealing across cultures (Chapter 9). The Applied Assertiveness Workshop (Chapter 10) takes you through some exercises in assertiveness to enable you to apply it in your work.

PART I

2 *Concepts*

Assertiveness means:

- being in charge of yourself

- being a good leader

- keeping calm in a crisis

- staying cool under fire: coping with criticism

- enjoying your successes: making the most of positive feedback

- setting your own limits: balancing health and commitment

- listening well: understanding the wants and needs of others without being pressurised

- communicating well: stating your own needs and wants without aggression

People under pressure tend to react in one of four different ways:

- directly aggressive

- indirectly aggressive

- passive

- assertive

As you will work on learning to recognise these types of behaviour, you will realise of course that it isn't only other people who are aggressive, passive or assertive under pressure, it is you as well. Some of the things you notice about yourself may not impress you! However, recognising what is going on is the first stage in improving things, so do not feel negative about what you discover: use it instead as an opportunity to develop.

Characteristics   The directly aggressive reaction is the one which responds with explosive anger to a difficult situation. It is quite different from assertive anger, and is not likely to lead to a good outcome.

DIRECTLY AGGRESSIVE BEHAVIOUR

Direct aggression is signalled by:

- refusal to listen

- shouting

- using intimidating body language

- interrupting

- using obvious put-downs

- swearing

Intimidating body language includes table-thumping, finger-pointing, stamping, and also invading someone's personal space by looming over them.

   A person reacting aggressively wants to win an encounter at all costs and wants the other person to lose. He or she is not looking for a win-win solution and will use all the means at his or her disposal to undermine the other person and avoid hearing any points they want to make by interrupting, overriding, shouting down and upsetting them.

Doing it   How does it feel to behave with direct aggression? At times it may feel like a relief, as though you are getting something out of your system. However, really getting something out of your system requires a more respecting and self-respecting assertive style. Losing your temper and being directly

Loss of control

aggressive can be a real loss of control. You are behaving without respect towards the person you are dealing with, but in doing that you lose your own self-respect as well, which is why so many people report feeling shame and guilt after an outburst of temper, as well as disappointment with themselves. Physically, people describe increased heart rate, increased sweating, deeper breathing and, in extreme cases, shaking and trembling during an aggressive outburst. All of these are normal and sometimes useful responses to stress. However, the negative after-effects of being aggressive in the work-place are that you may feel embarrassed at the time by your obvious agitation, and feel shaken and restless for several hours afterwards, with poor concentration and a real risk of making errors because your attention has been distracted.

Negative after-effects

Direct aggression is often directed not at the person who triggered it, but at a more junior person, or a person who is available when the person who triggered it is absent, as in the following example.

A personnel officer in a local government office said:

'I came out of a steering committee meeting, at which I had been, I thought, insulted. I did not manage to say or do anything about this except feel upset. I then came across two of the girls laughing and joking in the tea room long after I thought their tea break should be over and I went completely bananas, I really **yelled** at this poor girl – who handled it pretty well once she got over her amazement – just said she didn't think she'd overrun her break but she'd go back to her screen straight away. I felt absolutely dreadful though – I had actually come out in pink blotches which I saw in the mirror when I went to the Ladies to attempt to calm down. I was most embarrassed, and knew I had been completely unfair, but the worst thing was knowing that I had, for that few minutes, quite lost control of myself.'

This person ended up ashamed of herself and no further forward on her problem issues. The appropriate action would have been either to express her assertive anger to the person it really belonged to, or, if that was impossible, to be careful to offload it consciously to a speaking partner (see p. 55) or trusted friend. The assertive step forward when you have off-loaded aggression inappropriately like this is to take time to apologise without rolling in the dirt.

Aggressive outbursts may be linked with worry or pain in the person's family life. These worries might put everything into a heightened perspective, leaving him or her feeling very upset about apparently trivial matters, resulting in quick-temperedness followed by guilt and anxiety. A more assertive course – and a good use of 'yin' energy in the form of blending, sharing, and cooperative activity – might be to explain to colleagues, if possible, that there are problems outside of work.

Aggression can reveal much more about your feelings than you wanted or intended. The lawyer in this example had plenty to be angry about, but regretted exposing his feelings:

> 'I was sent away on a six-month secondment and when I got back there had, in effect, been a coup and there was no longer a job for me. When I was told this I lost my temper pretty comprehensively and in fact was glad that I didn't hit the person telling me. I certainly felt as though I might. My normal philosophy of life is "don't get mad, get even" – what they did to me was so dreadful, I would very much have preferred just to walk coldly away. I'm not happy that I let him see just how upset I was.'

And aggression about mistakes, delays and misunder-standings, is a great turn-off.

> 'As I shouted at him, which I know was not the right way to handle it, I saw his look grow sort of sullen underneath. Even though he's worked for me for months, I felt him get remote.'

Feeling directly aggressive, then, often feels embarrassing, disruptive and risky. Lastly, it often feels frustrating, since it rarely solves anything.

Being on the receiving end   Ask yourself how it feels to be on the receiving end of aggressive behaviour. You feel:

- threatened

- angry

- resentful

- scared

- secretive

- vengeful

Ask yourself how useful those feelings are within a working team. Remind yourself of specific times when you have felt this way yourself or observed colleagues feeling this way after an aggressive attack from someone. The ramifications within the team are almost always negative. True, a team sometimes needs shaking up or tightening up, or needs to be made to face up to mistakes or sloppiness, and it might seem that aggression is the most effective way to do it; but actually the cost of uncontrolled aggression is too high.

If you think you are going to get shouted at, one of the things you do is get out of range, either physically or emotionally. You can hardly be a committed team member if you are protecting yourself from the next explosion.

Anyone who feels threatened and scared is not going to work well. They will be afraid to report problems and mishaps to a manager who they perceive to be aggressive because they are frightened that he or she will fly off the handle. Thus any problems may get far worse before you even get to hear about them. Your staff will tend to become secretive.

The feelings of resentment will create in staff a need to 'get their own back' on the aggressive manager – which again is hardly conducive to a productive and effective team. Once you consider the true effects of aggression within a group of people it becomes less and less desirable as a way of managing. *Assertive* anger will do the trick far more effectively.

INDIRECT AGGRESSION

Indirect aggression may be harder to spot, but its effects are as destructive in a manager's relationship with his or her staff as those of directly aggressive behaviour.

Characteristics   You can recognise indirectly aggressive behaviour from one or more of these characteristics:

- moodiness

- sarcasm

- manipulative behaviour

- unexplained sighing, door-slamming, etc.

- creation of uneasy atmospheres

- inconsistency – being pleasant to your face and poisonous behind your back

- tantrum-throwing

- emotional blackmail

When you can tell that something's wrong but you don't know exactly what, or you find yourself feeling guilty or uncomfortable but you don't exactly know why, or someone's whole demeanour leaves you uneasy, but you can't quite pin down what it is that makes you feel that way, you're probably on the receiving end of indirect aggression.

Any body language or behaviour that makes for a tense atmosphere is indirectly aggressive, and so is the use of sarcasm to make a point instead of straightforward statement. (You may sometimes feel it is an advantage to be able to sting someone into action with a sarcastic comment, but the cost in loss of mutual trust is almost always going to be more than that particular issue is worth.)

Emotional blackmail (also known as 'management by tantrum') is indirectly aggressive, implying as it does, 'if you don't do what I want I shall be upset/angry/throw a wobbly of some sort'. Violet Elizabeth of the William books exemplified this manoeuvre in her frequent declarations 'I'll scream and I'll scream till I'm sick – and I **can** you know!' Consider whether you have colleagues who sometimes play things this way, and, of course, notice the times when you've done it yourself – there will almost certainly be some.

Doing it   How does it feel to **be** indirectly aggressive? As with direct aggression, many people report a degree of shame and self-disgust. It is not a practice that increases your self-respect; indeed it does quite the opposite, leaving a nasty taste of self-degradation.

Shame

It also feels very tense, because you are giving unclear messages and relying on others to decode them, which they may not successfully do. Thus you are not really in control of the content of what you are saying; you are relying on the other person to intuit it correctly. Of course you remain tense while you wait to see whether they do so or not.

Tension

An assertiveness course delegate said:

'I have never had the label "indirect aggression" to slap on this sort of behaviour before, but I do recognise doing it, and how it feels to me is tense, very, very tense. I feel very bottled up. When I come into the office and find that things that I wanted done are not done, yes I do sigh and slam doors and make sarcastic remarks; I'm just so pissed off.'

This person needs to find an assertive way to express dissatisfaction: he feels uncomfortably tense and his staff do not specifically know what they are doing wrong.

The other cause of tension in indirectly aggressive behaviour is that you are trying to control the other person through your emotions: you are threatening them with an emotional outburst of some kind if they don't comply with your wishes. The staff of an entertainment complex find their boss hard to cope with because of her indirect aggression, usually expressed in stinging sarcasm. One says:

'We really could do with a weather forecast because how your day is going to be depends directly on how Ellen's mood is. She blows hot and cold. On a good day she's as nice as pie, on a bad one you'd better watch out. I think we all resent how her moodiness rules our lives.'

Now, sooner or later, anyone treated with indirect aggression may call your bluff, and react assertively instead of passively. Tension arises from the anxiety that this may happen.

Isolation

Another consequence of being indirectly aggressive is feeling isolated. If you are not being straight with your colleagues, if you are charming to their faces and horrible behind their backs, if you make them subject to the vagaries of your moods, they will not like you much and will not single you out for socialising or confidences. You may become rather lonely.

Being on the receiving end   Receiving indirect aggression, one feels:

- confused

- frustrated

- resentful

- hurt

- outraged

- resistant

Take confusion first. What on earth is this person getting at? What exactly **do** they want you to do? Do they think you are up to the job, or not? Have you inadvertently said or done something appallingly tactless or stupid? And so on. This is what is going on is someone's head if they are subjected to indirect aggression. What a waste of time and energy.

An office manager makes this observation:

'I did not realise how much effect X's indirect aggression was having on me until it stopped. My office was moved to a different floor from his, and I'm aware how pleasant it is to be away from his whole atmosphere – the wondering what mood he's in, the wondering where he's going and what he's doing and what conspiracy is going on. I feel a whole lot more relaxed being right away from him.'

Think over any times you have felt this way yourself, and also any times when you have noticed colleagues in this state. Confusion like this is negative for the manager, for the staff and for the company, and is a strong reason for avoiding indirect aggression altogether.

The sense of frustration arises from the confusion. Since you do not know clearly what you are supposed to have done wrong, or what you are supposed to be doing next, you can't be confident that anything you do is the right thing.

Hurt and resentment are natural reactions to being manipulated and 'messed around' and indeed lead eventually to outrage and resistance, where you no longer even want to cooperate.

A third possible negative response to stress and challenge is to lapse into passive behaviour. When we are passive we exonerate ourselves from responsibility by throwing in the towel, and the pose we adopt is the pose of the victim.

PASSIVE BEHAVIOUR

Characteristics The presence of one or more of these behaviours signals passive behaviour:

- martyrish attitude
- self-pity
- low energy
- lack of ideas
- whining
- special pleading
- depressive body language

When we are in a passive state we have, essentially, given up responsibility for ourselves and our actions. It is at these times that we feel the whole world is against us, that whatever we do is bound to fail, and that therefore, in the last analysis, there is little point in making any effort with anything any more. Whenever you notice yourself saying or thinking –

'Why do these things always happen to me?'

or

'I might have known that would never work.'

or similar sentiments, you know you are moving into the passive mode.

A manager who works in telecommunications connected with this description of himself:

'Yes, there are times when I am passive. I would identify it as days or moods where I can't get off first base. At the first difficulty I can't see how to proceed, so I just stop and try to find something else to do and at the first problem with that I stick as well, and so it goes on all day.'

There are times of personal or professional crisis when it is appropriate to feel self-pity, and to need to use special pleading: for time off or extended deadlines for reasons of personal problems for example, or for extra support if a project of yours has, unexpectedly, gone disastrously wrong. This indicates passivity only if it becomes a habit, if you are regularly looking for a way out of your normal responsibilities with reasons that begin:

'I can't help it, because . . .'

'It's very difficult for me at the moment because . . .'

and so forth.

Depressive body language is usually characterised by slumping, be it backwards, forwards or at an angle!

Doing it   The pay-off in being passive is that it gets you, temporarily, off the hook. While you feel passive you certainly don't feel as though you can have any effect on anything that's going on.

Powerlessness

The costs, as with direct and indirect aggression, may on the other hand be seen to override this plus, because nearly all the other feelings associated with being passive are negative. It feels powerless being passive, and in fact it feels boring: if you are not really engaged with the work you are doing and have essentially given up on it, it becomes extremely tedious and the time drags. When asked to think about how passive episodes have felt in retrospect, people often report feeling confused about why it happened, and feeling disappointed in themselves.

Being on the receiving end   The team whose manager is behaving passively feels:

- demotivated

- lacking in confidence

- envious of other teams

- let down

- low in energy

- bored

- restless

When the person supposed to be giving you direction appears to have lost direction, your loyalty to the team, the plan, the vision, everything about the organisation, disintegrates. Staff are lost to organisations just as often through their manager being too passive as they are through their manger being too aggressive, because disillusion sets in and they lose faith in anything ever getting done.

When you are working around someone whose behaviour is predominantly passive, you feel your energy drain away and your own attitude being drawn towards passivity too.

ASSERTIVE BEHAVIOUR

In contrast to these three rather negative reactions to challenge or stress there is the assertive model of behaviour. It is a level-headed and honest manner where difficulties which must be confronted are confronted, and information which must be exchanged is exchanged, even if it is uncomfortable or difficult to do so.

Assertiveness is a mode of behaviour based on real self-esteem: there is both respect for oneself and respect for the other person, and a desire for the best solution to a problem rather than for a personal victory.

Characteristics   Assertive behaviour is signalled by:

- steady, pleasant voice pattern

- good eye contact

- relaxed body language

- ability to listen

- facing up to issues

- making your own needs and wants clear

- accepting refusals without panic

Doing it   An assertive person is at home with him or herself
and speaks and moves relaxedly and easily. He or she can work
out quickly what they want to say or do – the point they want to
make in a given situation or the outcome they want to support.
An assertive person accepts the fact that they sometimes make
mistakes, accepts that they sometimes need to ask for
information or assistance, and accepts the fact that their
requests are sometimes refused.

Being on the receiving end   Above all, those dealing with an
assertive manager feel they **know where they stand**. Working
and coexisting with someone who is assertive you feel:

- well-informed

- listened to and considered

- adult-to-adult (you can take care of yourself and they will
  take care of themselves)

- free to make suggestions

- free to take initiatives

- prepared to discuss mistakes

Because you are not under emotional pressure to behave like
a child being told off (if treated aggressively) or a parent making
everything come out right (if treated passively) you are free to
engage in adult-to-adult give and take, where good news and
bad can be shared equally, and action planning either way can
be done without recriminations or hysteria.

This line manager had not resolved some long-term
production problems. Her boss took it up with her assertively.
She says:

> 'I was taken aback at first that he was so direct about the
> problems I've been having in my section. On the other hand,
> we've faced up to things now. I suppose it was better than
> glossing over it.'

It can be a great relief when someone is assertive:

> 'Finally she said, if it isn't selling, we've got something wrong
> with the product. It was in the end a relief that someone at
> the meeting would be frank, although it wasn't particularly

pleasant to hear. Now, I thought, we'll have to really get down to it.'

Consider any times when you have been assertive, stood your ground in a strong, relaxed way, or dealt with a mistake without losing your dignity, and recall how it felt and what the outcome was. Remember also how it feels when bosses or colleagues have treated you assertively.

There are two costs in assertive behaviour. The first is that someone feeling very low in confidence may perceive it as overwhelming if you are assertive with them. This may happen more frequently when the person being assertive is a woman, because assertive women regularly, for cultural reasons, have to deal with being perceived as aggressive. However, since active listening and sensitivity are an important part of assertiveness technique, it is possible to adjust so as not to overwhelm anybody else.

The other cost is that, once you get into assertive mode, you have accepted your responsibility as an adult in the circumstances in which you find yourself. You can, however, console yourself with the thought that you are not taking inappropriate responsibility for anybody else in this mode.

When you put the checks and balances together, these two costs are far outweighed by all the good things which can grow from an assertive style, in the relationship between both managers and directors, and managers and staff.

The diagram on p. 20 should help clarify in your mind how the four types of behaviour relate to one another.

Pros and cons

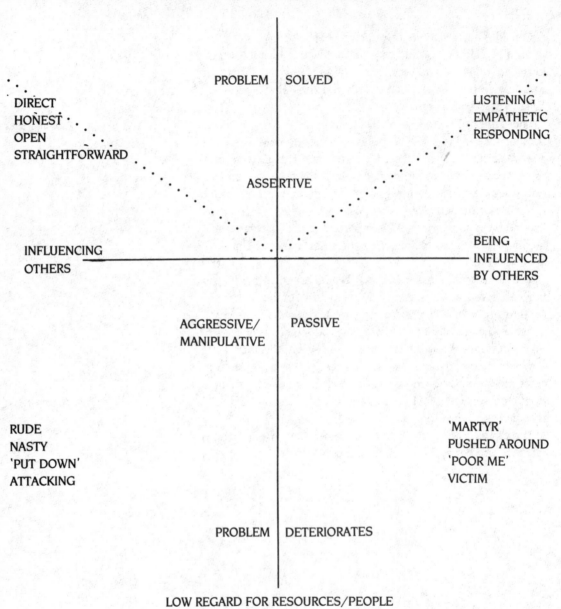

HIGH REGARD FOR RESOURCES/PEOPLE

PROBLEM | SOLVED

DIRECT
HONEST
OPEN
STRAIGHTFORWARD

LISTENING
EMPATHETIC
RESPONDING

ASSERTIVE

INFLUENCING
OTHERS

BEING
INFLUENCED
BY OTHERS

AGGRESSIVE/
MANIPULATIVE

PASSIVE

RUDE
NASTY
'PUT DOWN'
ATTACKING

'MARTYR'
PUSHED AROUND
'POOR ME'
VICTIM

PROBLEM | DETERIORATES

LOW REGARD FOR RESOURCES/PEOPLE

How the behaviours work psychologically can be neatly
summarised as follows:

Directly aggressive } Indirectly aggressive }	POWER OVER
Passive	OVERPOWERED
Assertive	POWER WITHIN

The aim of the work you do with this book is to be less and less
overpowering or overpowered, and more and more working from
the good basis of power within.

3 *Method*

*W*E will now move one from the 'what' of assertiveness to the 'how'. This chapter will present a range of specific techniques that can be built up into an overall management style. They are:

- active listening

- the core phrase

- the appropriate body language

- sharing empathy

- how to avoid 'hooks'

- the fallback position

ACTIVE LISTENING

Active listening creates a good two-way assertive communication, and therefore good problem-solving and effective planning.

Active listening means being alert and attentive to the other person while they speak, but not interposing your own ideas and interpretations until they have fully expressed what they want to say. It means learning how to interrupt only when it is constructive and necessary to do so. Good active listening may also include prompting the other person to summarise their idea or message when they have finished explaining it: this often helps to get to the real point of a problem or suggestion.

Active listening is characterised by:

- relaxed body posture

- relaxed intermittent eye contact

- smiles and nods as appropriate to encourage the speaker

- making a mental summary (or notes) of their main points as they go along

For someone to feel you are genuinely hearing what they say, you must be relaxed and alert, avoid fidgeting and paper-shuffling, and make enough eye contact to stay in touch without intimidating them. Nods, 'yes' and 'mm', and smiles will prompt or encourage the speaker to continue, but space them out or you will seem bored or patronising.

Collect in your own mind the main points of what is being said, either marshalling the points mentally, or making short notes. This prepares you when the person finishes speaking, to say,

> 'So what you're suggesting is (a), (b), and (c) – is that correct?'

Or, if you want them to sum it up, you can say,

> 'Right, what is the most important thing for me to take in about what you've said?'

This will usually prompt a useful pointer to their chief concern, and you can compare it with your own summary.

If someone is telling you something very difficult with a great deal of hesitation, ensure that they have an opportunity to say everything they want to say with the prompt,

> 'Is there anything else you'd like to add to that?'

when they seem to have finished. Sometimes the most important things don't come out till then.

Necessary interruptions are of three kinds:

- to stop material that is unacceptable or offensive

- to stop someone who is beginning to repeat themselves

- to re-interrupt when you have been interrupted

Learning good listening

Re-interruption is described in Chapter 5 on meetings, which is where this skill is needed most. If you are aggressively interrupted at a meeting, this is what you need to do to bring the discussion back to where you feel it ought to be. Find it on pp. 77–8.

Necessary interruption becomes part of active listening when the other person says things which are not acceptable or begins to behave in a way which is not acceptable. If they begin to speak in a sexist or racist manner, or become abusive or foul-mouthed, it is assertive and sensible to interrupt with:

'I must ask you to stop right there. What you are saying [or doing] is not acceptable. Now let's continue without [sexism, racism, swearing] and I'm listening carefully to what you have to say.'

Necessary interruption is also an acceptable part of active listening when the person talking begins to repeat themselves. When discussing a problem or describing an idea, many people speak in a spiral pattern where they almost finish, then go back to the beginning and repeat much of the material, almost finish, then return to the beginning again. This wastes their time and yours, and if it is a group meeting wastes the time of the meeting. It makes everyone but the speaker very tense.

Understanding interruption   Interrupt with the summarising prompt:

'Alright, let me stop you there. It seems to me that the main points you are making are (a), (b) and (c). Is that correct?'

If they respond by re-entering the spiral, interrupt again, and assert the summary:

'That's fine. Now the main points under discussion here are (a), (b) and (c)

– and lead straight into your answer or reaction,

'What I suggest we do is . . .'

Good active listening, for most of us, means learning to interrupt less. It means not leaping in with our own ideas until we are sure we have heard clearly what the other person is saying; it means being prepared to leave pauses while one or other of you thinks; it means having enough power within to let someone else have the floor without feeling you are losing control.

THE CORE PHRASE

The core phrase is at the heart of assertiveness technique. It is a clear, simple, direct and unequivocal phrase which expresses what you want to say. Staying with the core phrase helps you to make your point as effectively as possible, and fixes that point clearly in both your own mind and the mind of the person you are speaking with.

Evolving the core phrase clarifies your own purpose and determination. Decide what message *you* want to get across, and put it into a short, simple, positive phrase.

To make a good core phrase, you need to learn to avoid padding your statements out. Padding is the extra material which we use out of embarrassment or tension to elaborate around a point which feels stressful to tackle. It tends to undermine what we really intend to say. If you say,

Avoid padding

'I hope you don't mind me saying this, it feels a bit odd, but I just want to say how well I think you did that.'

you have trebled the length of the message and diluted its impact by about the same proportions. If you say,

'Well of course I'm always willing to try to help but I don't think I can do anything for you this time. Will you manage all right?'

it's difficult to work out that you are saying 'no', and furthermore, it sounds as though, with a bit more pressure, you might give in anyway. All that was needed was, in the first case,

Keep to the point

'That was terrific. Well done!'

and in the second,

'No, that won't be possible.'

A rather common form of padding in the UK is to say 'sorry' or 'I'm sorry' inappropriately to punctuate or introduce remarks or instructions:

Don't say 'sorry'

'Sorry, could you just move your chair please.'

(You do not need the 'sorry' or the 'just'.) It gives one's speech an apologetic and unvigorous tone. It is interesting to make a decision to say 'sorry' only when you actually want to apologise.

Sometimes we spin out sentences with extra words in order to gain time to think. It is often more effective to say, 'Give me a few minutes [or half an hour, or a couple of days, whatever is appropriate] to consider that and come back with an answer' – and come back with a concise core phrase when you are ready.

Usually, though, padding is a reflection of hesitancy about making the statement. With practice it is possible to evolve a core phrase without padding and to use it without padding, and thus to overcome the hesitation and make a strong statement. **A 'core phrase' may be very brief:**

'It's important that we meet as soon as possible . . .'

'This work really is not up to standard . . .'

'We need to finalise plans for the seminar today . . .'

'Please don't take that file home again . . .'

or it may grow into a paragraph if the message needs to contain several clear points.

For example, let's look at an item from one manager's 'agenda list':

'Sort out a junior who is claiming inside knowledge and spreading disruptive rumours among the others.'

The message

What is the message which must be conveyed? The exact content and emphasis depend of course on the particular case, but let us suppose that you want to communicate that:

(a)   you are aware of what he's doing,
(b)   it's destructive to morale, and
(c)   it's got to stop immediately.

Conveying it assertively

To put it assertively, you might say:

'I understand that you have spread some untrue rumours which have upset the other people in your section. You must stop this at once.'

These short sentences say everything you need to say, clearly, in a firm, assertive tone. They are unlikely to provoke a time-wasting argument, and can be returned to in order to reinforce the point if the staff member *does* dispute your statement.

An aggressive response

It is useful to look at what could have happened if you had gone into a directly aggressive mode, which you might well have done in such an aggravating situation:

'How dare you start these rumours? Who on earth would believe an idiot like you would have inside information anyway? You may think you're pretty clever, but you'd better watch out if you think you can get away with this kind of thing. Now get out.'

In this case you have said a number of things which may lead to irrelevant arguments and made a vague threat which cannot be upheld because it isn't specific. The staff member may go away rattled and upset, but:

(a)   has not necessarily taken in what precisely you object to,
(b)   has not necessarily taken in the fact that you want and expect an immediate stop to the behaviour, and
(c)   has no space to make any reply if there is a genuine point he needs to make.

It is useful too to think what might have happened if you approached the staff member reluctantly and in a passive mode. Perhaps it is someone you normally get on well with, and you feel awkward about expressing dissatisfaction with him; or perhaps you particularly dislike any kind of disciplinary activity.

A passive response

'Look Colin, I don't want to be unfair, and I am not really sure that what's been happening is your fault, but I do hear that there's a lot of negative talk in your section and that it is wasting a lot of time. Well it seems to be stemming mainly from you, is that true?'

In this case you used a lot of padding, did not clearly confront him with the problem, and did not make any mention of the fact that you want the behaviour to stop. You handed over all the power to him with your evasive phraseology and by finishing with a weakly expressed question.

The use of the extended core phrase, which gave the necessary messages clearly and unequivocally, is without doubt more effective.

Our short, clear core phrase functions most effectively when the body language and quality of voice which accompany it are right, reflecting accurately the content of what you are saying.

BODY LANGUAGE

Consider how *inappropriate* body language quickly undermines what you are trying to say.

'*Yes, that'll be fine*', said with a scowl, gives a message that negates the words.

'I*'m looking forward to it'*, deadpan, with a quarter turn to the left as you pick up the next file, doesn't ring true.

'I*'m really very angry about this'*, accompanied by an embarrassed grin, will not make much impact.

Body language can be divided into:

- proxemics
- stance
- gesture
- facial expression
- personal style

PROXEMICS

From the same word as 'proximity', proxemics is about where you are physically in relation to the people you are dealing with. It is a concept studied carefully by personnel such as the police who find themselves in situations which can easily get out of hand if they are not able to control the people around them, preferably with no physical contact at all.

In management, proxemics comes into its own because of the dual roles of reporting up and delegating down, in both of which the balance of power is critical.

We need to get into the habit of being aware of how close or far away our interlocutor is, our relative height and comfort, and also, sometimes, how the room is arranged.

Too far away

If you feel the person you are dealing with is uncomfortably far away from you, take an initiative and move closer, even if it means moving a chair or shifting other objects. If it's a bit of a performance to do so, 'report' what you are doing as you do it:

'You seem a long way away over there. I'm just going to transfer all the paperwork to this bit of the table and use this chair instead.'

Too close

Most of us have an invisible boundary of space around us into which we allow only people to whom we feel really close. This is our **personal space**. If someone unwelcome comes into our personal space we feel stressed, pressurised and invaded. If you are dealing with someone who is too close physically for comfort, move decisively away. It is not difficult to do this once you have realised that your discomfort is valid and rational, and that you do have a choice.

Touching another person is a delicate matter. There are cultural differences between North and South, between different ethnic groups, between Southern European and Northern European, between women and men, and within different professions, as to whether hand-shaking, kissing, back-slapping, hand-on-shoulder, arm-round-shoulder, and so on, are acceptable or not.

Appropriate touch

For example, the forms of touch welcome and acceptable in a theatrical company may be very different from those acceptable in a lawyer's office or a pharmaceutical laboratory, for a whole range of social and practical reasons. It is particularly important for a woman to feel that she can, with complete confidence and dignity, choose not to be touched if she does not want to be. Patting and stroking of a sort that, if she cried 'harassment', would be decried as minor have been part of an insidious disempowering of women in the workplace for years.

If someone is touching you in a way you do not like, you can move away, or if necessary you can say something like,

'I'm really not comfortable with that. Please don't do it.'

You always have the right to choose who touches you.

If you have made a mistake and touched someone in a way that they make clear is not comfortable for them, of course it is embarrassing, but you can apologise assertively, and show you respect their feelings.

'I'm so sorry, I didn't mean to impose on you.'

Relative height is of importance in keeping control of your own power. It is difficult to be assertive if your neck is craning back to address someone much taller than you, or if you are sprawled in a low chair while the other person is poised in an upright desk chair. So, if you are talking to someone much taller than you, invite them to sit down, and sit yourself down somewhere where your eye contact will be more or less level. If you are at an uneven height although you are both sitting down, get up and find a comfortable standing position or change chairs – either make no comment or report what you're doing:

Relative height

'That feels really uncomfortable, I'm going to move.'

The few seconds it takes to assess the proxemics as you enter a room are well worth taking. Train yourself to raise your awareness about closeness and distance, appropriate touch and relative height whenever you begin a transaction of any kind.

STANCE AND THE 'TANDEN'

On the whole managers are people who are rewarded for their head-work. Their importance is based in their ability to think analytically and act logically. There is, therefore, a real risk that they will come to use their bodies as simply something to support their head.

Bodies are, in fact, highly expressive. We cannot avoid that. What we can do is try to make sure they are expressing what we want them to: and in terms of assertiveness, this means making sure the stance matches the words.

Good **guidelines** for physical stance while being assertive are these:

- keep the back of the neck long

- make space between the ears and shoulders

- keep the distance between the sternum (breastbone) and the pubic bone long

- keep equal weight on each foot if standing, or each hip if sitting

Don't hunch

The first two points address the fact that once one becomes tense the back of the neck contracts and the shoulders tend to tense and hunch up. This can easily look aggressive – it emphasises the upper body musculature and the physical attitude typical of aggression. Consciously elongating the back of the neck and dropping the shoulders counteracts those effects.

Don't slouch

The third point looks at the fact that – as you can find out immediately by trying it – when one is tired, demoralised or enervated, the soft front surface of the body often collapses: one tends to hunch over and squash up the front of the body. This looks passive: it is typical victim body-language. If you stretch up and open the front of the body you avoid a defeated look.

Don't lean

The equal balance helps to keep the body symmetrical, counteracting a tendency in a pressurised situation to lean to one side or the other. Asymmetrical body postures generally indicate lack of confidence, and may signal either passive or indirectly aggressive behaviour.

Be strong but relaxed

There is no set stance which is typical of assertiveness, but a kind of calm alertness, with a loose-limbed feel to it is probably best. Think of your joints being flexible and loose, and your muscles being strong but relaxed. Think of your lungs, your heart and your digestive system working well and without strain! If they do not, give some honest thought to why. Any of those vital systems being stressed or painful is a signal that your life is pushing your body into a state it does not want to be in. We all have to override some of those signals sometimes, but to override strong physical signals of distress continually is asking for trouble. If your body has something to say to you, listen to it.

One further point on assertive stance is this:

● keep your weight based low in your body.

'No problem!' you may reply if your figure is beginning to reflect the effects of too many corporate lunches in an increasing hip measurement. However, keeping your weight low is a different thing from keeping your fat low.

There is an interesting parallel here with martial arts training. To be really powerful in the fighting arts, you keep your centre of gravity in your hips – the place is called 'tanden' (Chinese), 'tan-tien' (Japanese), or 'danjun' (Korean), and is three finger-breadths below the navel. It is over this place that the martial artist's belt is tied, and many oriental ceremonial uniforms feature a decorative belt which emphasises the 'tanden', where as in the West we tend to have elaborate headgear, emphasising cerebral activity, or epaulettes, which emphasise upper body strength. The body is more stable, more mobile, more fluent, if you can move your centre of gravity, your feeling of where your power and energy come from, down from head or heart level to the 'tanden'. Try gradually to become aware of this, and get a sense of your physical and emotional strength being, literally, at gut-level.

Keep centre of gravity low

To manage the strong, relaxed body language which is the best physical back-up to verbal assertiveness, living more fully in your body is helpful. Any form of exercise which keeps you lively, flexible and in touch with your physical self is going to enhance your ability to be assertive, and therefore your performance at work. That applies to 'unofficial' exercise like gardening, walking, making love, or playing riotous games with children, just as much as to 'official' exercise like squash, weight training, or swimming.

Exercise

Gesture is mainly what you do with your hands, arms, shoulders and head. The more integrated you are physically, the easier you will find it to use gesture unselfconsciously and fluently. This certainly adds power and interest to anything you say.

GESTURE

For many of us, though, the first step is to avoid the type of gestures we *don't* want to make. The increasing use of videotape

Control undesirable gestures

in management and presentation courses has given many of us a horrible insight into our hitherto unrecognised tendencies towards hand-twisting, hair-twirling, chair-tipping, writhing, and other unattractive gestural tics. All we can do after the initial hilarity or tears is to focus on calm alertness and begin to bring the gestures under control!

Keep hands still

It is sensible to keep your hands away from your face. It is easy to undermine an assertive message by obscuring bits of your face while you are saying it, and even by covering your mouth so that you almost seem to be holding the words in.

It is also worth learning not to fiddle with jewellery, pencils, paperclips, and so forth, while you talk. If you are giving a presentation using a flip chart, do not snap the lid on and off the flip chart pen as you speak! If your hands feel jittery and agitated, imagine exhaling out of your fingertips. Having done that, if your hands still feel tense, clasp them loosely together, and they will restrain each other.

Appropriate arm gestures

Generally speaking, if your hands and arms are open or outstretched it shows that you are open to what is being said, and an arms folded, chest constricted gesture shows that you are not. The open hand or open arms gesture can be useful if you are prompting someone who has something they are hesitating to say. However, closed gestures are not always negative. If someone is being very aggressive towards you, folding your arms loosely in front of you indicates that you are not prepared to be railroaded.

Getting rid of gestures that are distracting or inappropriate, and beginning either to learn to be still, or to see what sort of relaxed gestures come spontaneously, is more useful than learning a code of gestures as though it was a kind of semaphore.

FACIAL EXPRESSION

Videotaping may also have given you clues to whether your face matches your words when you speak. To make sure it does, relax your facial muscles (be aware of the centre of the brow, the muscles around the mouth and the muscles around the eyes) and then let your face follow what you are saying. If a situation is serious, an appeasing grin really does threaten your ability to control the situation. If you really want to appear concerned, it cannot be done if your face expresses boredom.

Match face to words

Steady but intermittent eye contact

Eye contact should be intermittent and light. Too much eye contact becomes aggressive, too little is passive. Eye contact intended to express things wordlessly is often indirectly aggressive (snide), or passive (pathetic or wheedling), or aggressive (glaring). To look at someone in a way that reinforces your assertive stance, a steady, straight gaze is needed.

How much is 'just the right amount' of eye contact? There isn't a 'correct' amount. It is something which is delicately and tacitly negotiated between the people in a discussion. One needs to heighten one's awareness of it and try to find the optimum.

It is particularly important not to break eye contact when a key word in the discussion arises. Given that you *are* breaking contact intermittently it is very difficult *not* to glance away when the crunch word or phrase is said. If you have to say,

Don't break eye contact on key words

> 'The rumours of your affair are disturbing the juniors and your time-keeping seems bad too. Your private life is your own, but when it interferes with professionalism I need to talk to you about it.'

– it is absolutely crucial *not* to look away on the words 'affair' or 'private life'.

If it is necessary to say,

> 'I've asked you to come in and see me because I have some bad news for you. Please sit down.'

– do not lose your eye contact on 'bad news'.

And if it is good news,

> 'The feedback from the customer was terrific. Good for you.'

– do not lose touch with the other person's gaze on 'terrific'or 'good for you'.

Clothes, shoes, hairstyle, briefcase, diary, all your choices of dress and equipment are also part of your non-verbal communication. The power-dressing games of the 1980s have given way to a more one-world-awareness distaste for conspicuous consumption – or blatant conspicuous consumption at least. The emphasis is on understated quality and subtler style: which is in fact very much easier for the manager to cope with in trying to make a good visual impression.

PERSONAL STYLE

To organise your own personal style, look at what seems culturally acceptable in your workplace: Is it all right for the men here to wear a pony-tail? Can the women in this organisation come to work in trousers? Have you got to wear a tie every day? If so, what range of colours is acceptable? And so forth. Your

Fit the corporate culture

early days in an organisation, and/or your early days of promotion into the managerial tier, are not the best times to throw down the sartorial gauntlet, unless you really want to put a lot of energy into that.

Try to choose **clothes** which:

● fit easily into the corporate culture, unless you consciously want to challenge it

● fit *you* well: do not hurt or pinch anywhere, no matter how you sit, move, or stand, climb into and out of cars, on and off platforms, and so on

● stay secure: do not come undone, adrift, need hitching up or down constantly, whatever you are doing

● have at least one thing about them that you positively like – cut, colour, texture, whatever, that makes them personally yours

● you can completely forget about 99% of the time knowing that they look appropriate and pleasant

The same goes for **hairstyles**. The ideal for men as well as for women is a hairstyle which one can forget because, so long as it is clean, it always looks good without endless ministrations in the form of blow-drying, gelling, etc. – again, unless hair rituals and investment are a positive pleasure to you.

Women in management face a particular challenge over physical appearance: being in a wider culture where they are under intense pressure to be thin and pretty on the one hand, and on the other being in a corporate culture where it may be extremely difficult for them to be taken seriously if thin and pretty, if that is what they happen to be, poses endless contradictions. The decade of bleak dark suits for senior women through the 1980s reflected that conflict, though there *is* a calmer flexibility growing in the 1990s.

Be at ease with your style

Women and men at ease with their own clothes and equipment – not feeling self-conscious because they look shabby, or silly because their clothes and briefcases are so expensive that they feel intimidated by them – will look good, capable, pleasant and reliable. This is a secure starting place for making sure your personal style backs up your assertive behaviour.

VOICE QUALITY

Just as many people are alienated from their bodies, many are disconnected from their voices, and don't express themselves powerfully by their voice quality.

Getting in touch with your voice, and developing it so that it works with you rather than against you, will improve your assertive performance. The three points to watch in voice quality are:

Get in touch with your voice

- speed

- pitch

- timbre

When one is anxious, one's verbal delivery tends to speed up. This has obvious disadvantages: it is more difficult to understand what someone is saying if they are speaking very quickly, and there is a real risk of missing important information if it is coming out very fast. Furthermore, someone talking very quickly sounds anxious, which does not give a powerful or positive impression.

Whenever you find yourself in a challenging or tense situation, think of slowing your voice down.

Slow down

Voice pitch is also affected by tension and stress. Most people's voices rise in pitch when they are under pressure, and this tends to drain authority away from what is being said. A delivery which is becoming squeaky is not very impressive!

As well as consciously slowing your speech down in order to remain assertive, think of pitching it low as well: remind yourself of the phrase 'lowish and slowish'.

Pitch low

Timbre is a more subtle quality than pitch and speed, but you will recognise it easily once you think about it. At our most expressive, our voices are quite full and resonant and come from the diaphragm or the belly. At our most rattled, unsure of ourselves and harassed, our voices are thin and come from the throat area.

Resonate

If you sing, even if only in the bath, you will know the feeling of the full voice coming from the diaphragm. If you do a sport where you are encouraged to make a noise, or one where it is part of the technique (like *kiai* in Karate, or *kiup* in Tae Kwon Do), you will also be familiar with this diaphragmatic voice.

The more resonance your voice has, the more steady and assertive authority it can carry. To encourage your voice to develop in fullness it is not necessary suddenly to become operatic! All that is necessary is to increase your awareness of where your voice is coming from, and, when you hear it thin and constricted in your throat, to reach down lower with it and bring it up from the diaphragm area. Take any opportunities you get to sing or shout with a full voice and an open throat.

You now know how to work out a core phrase and how to match it with consistent body language. The next stage is to show empathy and to learn how to avoid getting 'hooked' by irrelevant or unproductive argument.

SHOWING EMPATHY

This means being able to listen and respond to the other person's point without feeling pulled into their logic if you do not want to be, and without weakening your own determination. It also means responding fairly to a genuinely new point which you either had not known or had not realised before.

Mutual respect

Show that you have heard what the other person is saying by repeating some of it back to them with 'I see', or 'I realise' as a preface:

> 'I see how worried you are about how these cuts are going to affect your staff . . .'

> 'I understand that it's asking everyone to raise productivity . . .'

> 'I realise it's never been done this way before . . .'

> 'I understand that you've had problems at home . . .'

This empathy is an empathy of mutual respect, not of dissolving yourself into the other person's point of view. Further, it keeps the emotional temperature even: nothing is more infuriating than believing your manager is not listening to you. It is positive and calming to feel that they are listening.

AVOIDING 'HOOKS'

After clearly showing empathy, you can add the skill of avoiding 'hooks'. A hook is any kind of gambit that seems likely to pull you into an argument that is leading nowhere, or leading you away from your goal as encapsulated in your core phrase.

Hooks can be of various kinds:

- manipulative

- argumentative

- irrelevant logic

A **manipulative hook** is one which tries to make you feel guilty:

'We rely on you to run that training session. You know you're by far the best at it and you're really letting us down if you won't do it. Don't you have the best interests of the juniors at heart?

An **argumentative hook** tries to provoke you into a row:

'How could you make such a stupid suggestion?'

'What's the matter with you – I thought you had a sense of humour?'

A piece of **irrelevant logic** sounds rational but doesn't stand up to any real scrutiny:

'We've never done it that way before.'

'What if it doesn't work the way they said?'

'But I've arranged to play golf this afternoon.'

The way to respond is to show empathy and then to repeat your core phrase. 'Play back' all or part of what the other person said:

Not getting hooked

'I understand that you would like me to run that training course . . .'

– then add your core phrase:

'. . . but it's essential that I prioritise other work this month.'

'I realise you feel it's a stupid suggestion [playback/active listening] – but I think we should look at it seriously: it contains several important points [core phrase].'

'I understand that it's never been done this way before [playback/active listening] – but I think this new system is a real improvement [core phrase].'

'I see you feel I'm lacking in humour here [playback/active listening] – but I am making a clear complaint about harassment and I want you to listen [core phrase].'

'I understand that you've arranged to play golf this afternoon, [playback/active listening] – but there is a crisis in the marketing department, and I strongly feel you should be there to help sort it out [core phrase].'

Falling for a hook

Look at what could have happened if you *had* got hooked. With our first example it would have been all too easy to be caught either by the point 'You're letting us down' or by the point 'Don't you have the best interests of the juniors at heart?' You could have entered into a fruitless argument:

'How could you accuse me of letting you down after the hours I've put in over the last six months!'

or

'Of course I have the best interests of juniors at heart – you're so unreasonable and I really feel you're pushing me too hard.'

From there things can only escalate into an argument or meander off into pantomime:

'Oh yes, you did.'
'Oh no, you didn't.'

The risk with the provocative hooks is scripts beginning:

'Don't you accuse me of being stupid – who do you think you are?'

or

'There's nothing wrong with my sense of humour mate. You want to concentrate on being efficient, never mind wanting people to find things funny.'

or

'Why do you always have to be so bloody personally unkind? I can't take any more of it.'

and there's the pantomime too:

'Oh no, it isn't stupid.'
'Oh yes, it is.'

or

'Oh yes, I have got a sense of humour.'
'Oh no, you haven't.'

These are not useful options.

The risk with the irrelevant logic hooks is the sophistry you can get involved in. Do not waste time and energy on the fact that this is an innovation, or why everybody might or might not make golf of paramount importance. Stay with the active listening plus the core phrase.

FALLBACK POSITION

One last point of technique before we move on to practice and role play is establishing your fallback position. This has a similar function to setting a private upper limit on your bid at an auction: it prevents you being carried away in the heat of the moment and giving away more than you intended.

Not every assertive transaction is aimed at holding your beginning position completely right through to the end, without any changes. The aim rather is to be flexible and responsive to negotiation but to be clear what your boundaries are, and make only the changes to your position that you want to make.

When you analyse a 'problem scene' (see p. 43) it is useful to make a supplementary note on 'how far you will go' – i.e. your fallback position.

'If it's absolutely necessary, I will extend the deadline for another fortnight.'

'You can use some of our secretarial capacity now, but it's on condition that your section does the same for us in the rush at the end of the financial year.'

'If you really feel it's not viable for me to go away next week I will respect that, but I do need that training and I would like to book onto the course next time it runs.'

'You were quite mistaken in thinking I feel attracted to you. I'm prepared to forget the whole incident but I want to be quite clear it won't happen again.'

If you are negotiating on the telephone or in a large meeting where your own notes are not visible to others, you may like to make a note of your fallback position and check with it from time to time during your discussion. Face to face you must hold the fallback position clearly in your mind. Mentally refer yourself back to it at each challenge in the discussion. Check that you are negotiating as you really want to.

Sometimes an encounter arises or escalates suddenly and you have no chance to work out precisely what your fallback position is. If it is possible to do so, ask for time:

'Give me a few moments to consider this.'

If that gives away too much power, or is a practical impossibility, simply check at each point in the transaction whether you are still negotiating in a range within which you feel comfortable, or whether you are at risk of going too far. In this way you clarify your fallback position as you go along, even if you did not have a chance to work it out specifically.

You are now ready to try out these techniques yourself, and integrate them into your own style.

Putting it all Together: *Assertiveness Workshop* 4

A step-by-step development workshop will help you to check that you understand the concepts underpinning assertiveness, and will give you an opportunity to see how it meshes in with your own experience. You will also start trying out the techniques of assertiveness yourself. As you work through the steps, use the review chart at the end of the chapter to make notes.

STEP 1: RECOGNISING FOUR DIFFERENT TYPES OF BEHAVIOUR

Look at the following scenarios and decide which of the four types of behaviour you feel the reaction exemplifies. You can work through these alone, or in pairs, or they can be used for recognition practice in a group training exercise.

Situation	*Response*	*Your Answer*
A junior with personal problems has rung you at home to discuss them. It's important to you to keep the boundaries between home and work clear.	'Well I suppose I can give you 5 minutes now, but please remember I'm not the bloody Samaritans, OK?'	

continued

Situation	Response	Your Answer
Arriving at work one morning you find a colleague has taken your parking space without asking. You need to load your car with several heavy items of equipment and you have a split-second schedule which will now run at least 15 minutes late.	'How dare you take my parking space without asking! I've got three presentations to do which are a damn sight more important than anything you're likely to be doing today. What do you think you're playing at?'	
You're being pressed to have a drink mid-morning to celebrate a deal. You're delighted with the deal but know alcohol early in the day makes you feel lousy. The implication if you refuse is that you're a killjoy.	'No, I really don't want a drink now thanks. Many congratulations on a great success – and I'll drink your health later.'	
A crucial meeting has been called on a day you booked leave for a sporting event weeks ago.	'I suppose I'll pick up the drift when I get back. Don't do anything too important without me, will you?'	
Cash flow this month looks terrible. Everybody must get as many cheques in as possible and you have to motivate your staff to do this.	'You so-called professionals are going to have to work for your money this month. I know it will seem a bit strange to some of you, but you'll just have to try.'	

STEP 2: SETTING YOUR OWN AGENDA

Take an overview of the last six months at work. Flick back
through your diary if that helps to remind you exactly what you
have been doing, and who you have been dealing with. Make a
list of between five and ten situations where you would have
liked (would still like, if it's an ongoing problem or relationship)
to be more assertive. Any occasion when you were not pleased
or satisfied with how you related to other people, how you coped
with challenges or negotiations, can go on your list. Choose
items which interest you or catch your attention at this moment.
They are catching your attention because they have an important
message for you now. Do not omit items because they seem
trivial. The incident itself may be trivial but it may represent an
important pattern for you, and it is unlikely that it would have
come into your mind if this was not the case.

List problem situations

This list can be entirely private, so you really can include
anything you like. Keep it, both to draw examples from in further
exercises in the book, and to review in six months' or a year's
time. You will be delighted to find that things you thought were
quite intractable when you made the list have shifted for the
better or even been completely resolved. The list is your
personal agenda of management matters where you would like
to be/would like to have been more assertive.

It might look something like:

1   Martin took all the credit for project X when really I did all
    the work on it. I let him walk all over me. I just could not
    think how to raise it without sounding pathetically petty.
2   I am completely fed up with client Y abusing me over the
    phone. I want to keep the client without submitting to being
    sworn at at length every couple of weeks.
3   I overheard two juniors making some overtly racist remarks
    in the coffee-making room last week. I'm too embarrassed to
    talk to them about it but I'm also (a) very angry, and (b)
    aware that I ought to be making sure this doesn't happen.
4   I lost my temper when the reports were out late again. I
    scared the wits out of the people concerned but I still don't
    know why they don't get them done in time.
5   I never feel I look right when I'm making presentations; I
    wish I could find somewhere decent to get my hair cut.
6   I really hate walking across the shop floor in my suit. I feel so
    self-conscious.
7   I've got to ring up a client and chase a bad debt. I'm
    dreading doing it.

8 I can't go on forever covering up the fact that I don't thoroughly understand the new software. I need to work out a way of asking for help without losing face.

9 I drink far too much.

This person's list includes quite personal things (I drink too much, I don't look right), disciplinary problems (racism, overdue work), interpersonal matters (he stole my thunder, he shouts at me unnecessarily), and future professional challenges (I dread making that call, I can't face trying to absorb this information). Your list may have a similar mixture, or an emphasis towards the technical, the interpersonal or the personal. Notice what your own emphasis is. This is your agenda for today. If you made a similar list next week or next month you would probably have other things on your mind, and some of the items would be different.

Note current responses

Your list describes times when you are not, at the moment, being assertive. Since that is the case, note by each item the way in which you are behaving now – i.e. directly or indirectly aggressively, or passively. It is quite common to want to put more than one label; for instance to note that you see-saw between aggression and passivity on some item. If that is the case, simply put both labels on.

Number problems in order of difficulty

The next operation is to number your points in order of difficulty, with the easiest one to improve or resolve being number one, and the more difficult ones being the higher numbers. The reason for doing this is that it is useful to start working in 'real life' on the lower-numbered easier issues, and get a good foundation by having successes with these, then to move on to the more difficult ones.

You may be tempted to start with the more difficult points since they are the ones which are depleting your managerial performance the most. But it is worth remembering that it is often more effective to gain some confidence by succeeding with the easier points, and to use that good experience to strengthen you for the tougher matters.

Keep your list somewhere private for future reference.

STEP 3: A BILL OF RIGHTS

If assertiveness means dealing with another person or a group of other people clearly, directly and on an equal-adult basis, then to use it effectively you need to work out what you consider to be a reasonable 'bill of rights' for all parties in any discussion.

Note down everything you think **you** are owed in an adult-to-adult assertive transaction, and take time to recognise the fact that, logically, if you think you are due these rights, then anyone you deal with is due them too. Notice any rights which you clearly want to claim for yourself, but feel ambivalent about according to others.

If you are organising training on assertiveness skills, the bill of rights exercise can be set as a group discussion activity. Divide your delegates into groups of four or so and ask them to evolve a bill of rights. After 15 minutes get each group to feed back. Ask them to report on any rights which any of their members feel ambivalent about, as above; and, further, ask them to report on any rights which were contentious. This provides a fruitful opportunity for colleagues to explore the underlying dynamics of a transaction, and any differences of opinion there may be among them about these.

Group discussion exercise

The bill of rights drawn up by such reflections and discussions may look something like this:

TOWARDS A 'BILL OF RIGHTS'

Everyone has the right:

1 to hold and express views that are different from other people's
2 to be listened to and be taken seriously
3 to say no
4 to disagree
5 to be treated with respect
6 to admit ignorance
7 to set their own priorities
8 to express anger
9 to privacy
10 to choose not to be assertive
11 to be wrong.

It is useful to stick your own version of the 'Bill of Rights' to your office wall where you can see it. If the exercise is set in a group training exercise, suggest that all delegates take a copy of their group's 'Bill of Rights' and do the same.

Building a positive picture **of** yourself **for** yourself is another vital part of the groundwork in becoming an assertive manager.

Remember the diagram on p. 20 – true assertiveness means having the real source of your power inside yourself. Consider what Kaleghl Quinn says in *Stand Your Ground*.

> We must be aware that when we lean or rely on others to make us 'feel good' about ourselves, we are also investing in the possibility of them making us 'feel bad' . . . it is fine to lean upon someone or something so long as there is a mutual agreement; but if you are leaning without knowing it then you will fall when that person or thing goes away.

For many of us, building self-esteem from within is a new idea. Many families, many schools and many corporate cultures condition us to expect assessment and positive feedback from outside superiors rather than from within ourselves. Particularly in the UK, a kind of ironic diffidence is expected from professionals.

Thus, developing a good base of self-esteem may mean running counter to the habits of a lifetime. Try this structured suggestion as a good way of beginning.

You can do this alone, or it can also be done very effectively in a training session in pairs. It must, however, be tried only in groups that are contracted to keep confidence, and in which the atmosphere is of mutual trust among the delegates. In pair work, one person speaks while the other listens well and supports, but does not interrupt or prompt at all.

List your strengths

Take 4 minutes (timed) to write, if you are working alone, or say, if you are working with a partner, a list of things which you are very good at. As many times as you can, complete the sentence:

'I'm very good at . . .'

This will seem a shocking thing to do at first! Do not worry if there are long pauses in between sentences; just keep going for the 4 minutes. Don't censor things which seem trivial, and if you find you are making the crossover between work and other parts of your life, include those things too. Resist the temptation to slide into, 'I'm quite good I suppose . . .'

One might expect this sort of list:

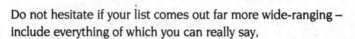

I'm very good on technical matters.
I'm very good at listening to people's problems.
I'm very good at catching deadlines.
I'm very good at jogging.
I'm very good at being cheerful in the mornings.
I'm very good at being a good friend.
I'm very good at getting things finished properly.

Do not hesitate if your list comes out far more wide-ranging –
include everything of which you can really say,

   'I'm very good at this.'

   If you are working in pairs, change roles so that the person
who listened speaks for 4 minutes, and the person who spoke
does the listening this time.
   When you have said or written the things which you are good
at, spend some time talking about/thinking over how it felt to
do this exercise. Share whatever feelings you have with your
partner (or write them down) – they may include
embarrassment, going blank, feeling upset, excited, surprised,
proud, whatever comes up for you. Notice whether it would have
been easier to speak or write for 4 minutes about your
shortcomings!
   This sense of the unique and interesting combination of things
that you as an individual are good at can be the basis for
'contacting your strength'.
   Review your list again: is there any one thing or cluster of
things which you feel particularly proud of? If so these can be
the focus of 'your strength'. If not, simply get an overview of the
whole lot.
   Remind yourself of your strength regularly, and before or
during a stressful or upsetting transaction get in touch with it by
reminding yourself specifically – 'I'm very good at [as many
things as you like]'. Once you get practised at doing this, you can
'contact your strength' easily and quickly, any time you need it.
It can become a touchstone for you.

Remember your strengths

STEP 5: ACTIVE LISTENING

You do need a partner for this exercise! You can work as a pair,
or it can be used as a pairs exercise in a staff training session.
One person is the speaker and the other is the listener. The

speaker has 4 minutes to talk through his or her thoughts on one of the following subjects:

- a recent success at work

- a recent problem at work

- how I use my spare time

- how I see the next five years for me

The listener does not interrupt, tries to follow the guidelines for active listening (p. 23) and stays alert and attentive.

After 4 minutes, change roles. When you have both experienced both roles, do the following:

1   Give the other person your main-points summary of what they said. Check it out with their view of what they said. How well did you listen and pick up on what was important to them?
2   Discuss how it felt to be listened to without interruption.
3   Discuss how it felt to listen without making interruptions.
4   Sum up to each other what you have learned from doing this exercise.

STEP 6: CORE PHRASE WORK

You can do this work on core phrases alone by making notes, or in a small group (three or four is ideal) within a training session.

Find the 'agenda list' which you made in response to Step 2. Choose an item on that list on which you would like to work. If you are working in a group choose an item which you are happy to discuss with the other people in your group.

1   Give a brief background to the item you are working on.
2   Work out the core phrase you need to use.
3   Practise saying your core phrase out loud.

Work out your core phrase

If you are working alone you must do 1 and 2 in written form. If you are in a group, they can help you to formulate the core phrase.

Say your core phrase aloud

It is useful to have other people to assist you through all you 'yes buts' and 'what ifs' and 'that would never work' reflexes. It is also useful to try out saying your core phrase to them. It is a surprisingly powerful experience to say clearly, in the outside air rather than in your head, something you have needed and wanted to say for some time:

'The chair in your office which I sit in for briefings is uncomfortably low. May I sit in this chair instead?'

'Since we are committed to saving paper, can I redesign these forms to fit onto one sheet?'

'I find this calendar offensive and I'd like you to remove it.'

'No, I don't want to become involved on that project.'

'We're never going to be great friends, but we have to work together. I'd like to do that on a basis of mutual respect.'

'There's an odd atmosphere in your section. Do you know what's bothering everybody?'

'I think we should face up to why we weren't even short-listed for that tender.'

'If we don't get the distribution better organised I am seriously worried about the consequences. I think we should prioritise that right now.'

When you have got that good core phrase correct, do not start elaborating on it, do not start explaining or making justifications, or giving extra data to back it up. You can do all those things later, as and when necessary. Even if the core phrase gets followed by a short, maybe even stunned, silence, just leave it hanging in the air, as your most powerful possible opening move.

STEP 7: PERSONAL STYLE

In pairs in a training session, or in written form if you are working alone, take 4 minutes to describe your favourite piece of clothing – the most favourite one you've ever owned. Say what it was, what it is you like or liked about it, and what it expressed about you. It could be something old or new or recycled, sporty or arty, shared with someone else, to do with your work, or some hobby, or some uniform. Take your time to decide which item really is your favourite, then talk about it and around it for the allotted time. Your partner listens actively without interrupting.

If you are working in pairs, change roles after 4 minutes and listen while your partner talks about his or her favourite piece of clothing.

After this, have some time together to discuss what you've learned from this exercise and what it tells you about which qualities you would really like in your personal style. Discuss whether there are any adjustments you would like to make to the way you dress for work that would make you feel more strongly 'yourself' and therefore more able to be assertive.

STEP 8: BODY AND VOICE EXERCISE

This exercise gives you an opportunity to become more aware of what your body and voice are doing when you speak aggressively, passively and assertively. It's very useful to do the exercise with at least one partner, and preferably in a group of 3 or 4, so that you can give each other feedback and comments.

Here are some short phrases which one often needs to say assertively:

'I'm not happy with this piece of work and I want it done again.'

'I've got a lot of work to get through and I don't want to chat now.'

'Well done! You managed that brilliantly.'

Say each of these phrases, with exactly the same words, in the following styles:

- directly aggressively
- indirectly aggressively (i.e. sarcastically or manipulatively)
- passively
- assertively

Mix the order up and see whether the other people in your group can tell which style you are using. Notice how your voice sounds and what position your body is in.

You may wonder whether, for example, it is possible to say 'Well done' aggressively, but when you try it you will find it is possible to inject considerable menace into even such positive words as those!

STEP 9: BREATHING WELL

Many managers suffer from feeling permanently rushed. Hurry and pressure can affect your breathing, usually producing a rather shallow, fast breathing pattern. If you learn to breathe deeply and slowly you can produce a much more resonant and powerful voice. You can also use the breathing as an aid to calming down when you begin to tense up.

When the overhead projector breaks down in an important presentation, when the train taking you to an urgent meeting stops inexplicably in the middle of nowhere, when you realise you have left your briefcase at the airport – learn to say to yourself '*breathe*!' Deliberately move into the breathing pattern described here. It will steady your emotions, and will enrich the supply of oxygen to your brain, so you will be better able to work out what to do next.

We can live for days without food, and for hours without water. We cannot live for more than a couple of minutes without breathing. How extraordinary it is that we never practise doing it better.

Breathing pattern

1   Sit with your spine straight, shoulders relaxed, and neck long. If you are in a chair, uncross your legs and place both feet on the floor. If you are sitting on the floor, cross your legs if you can comfortably.
2   Close your eyes. Place your left hand on your knee. Relax your hand. Place your right hand on your abdomen, below your navel. Do not fret about feeling fat – we are not concerned with that right now.
3   Start to breathe a little more deeply and a little more slowly than usual. Hear the breath as it comes and goes.
4   When you have got into a good rhythm, start to breathe in through your nose, and out through your mouth. Do not blow the breath out – just part your lips and let the air escape.
5   When you are breathing easily in through the nose and out through the mouth, begin to become aware of your hand on your abdomen. Direct your breath in down towards your hand, and feel your breath out coming all the way up from behind your hand.
   Breathing in, you fill up, so your abdomen swells into your hand a little.
   Breathing out, you empty, so your abdomen deflates a little.
   It is only a small change in the abdomen – do not puff it out and collapse it vigorously.
6   When you are breathing comfortably down towards the abdomen, in through the nose and out through the mouth, just add one more thing. Make a tiny hesitation between

each movement of the breath: breathe in, and hesitate; breathe out, and hesitate.

7   Continue with this deep, steady breathing as long as you want to. When you want to stop, move your right hand onto your right knee and relax it. Let your breathing return to an everyday level. Become aware of your surroundings before you blink your eyes open to let in the light.

8   Do not rush. Pause to appreciate the peaceful feeling you have created simply by altering your breathing. Take some of that peace with you into the next part of your day.

STEP 10: ASSERTIVENESS ROLE PLAY

In a training group you can do role play with a partner acting with you and a number of observers giving you feedback on what you are doing. If you do not have a group available to you it is still useful to do role play with a partner – someone you trust both to keep your confidentiality and to assist your development. Even if you are on your own it can be useful to practise saying your core phrase, to imagine all the possible hooks which might be thrown at you and how you would reply to them assertively, and to be aware what your fallback position is. Play it through to yourself as if it was a video of you managing the situation exactly as you would wish to, and notice your good body language and assertive skills. Such positive visualisations, far from being silly fantasising, are in fact rather powerful and help to develop in reality the behaviour which they picture.

Choose an item from your agenda on which you would like to work using role play. Explain the background briefly to your group and ask one or more of them to act the other people in the situation. Give them prompts and cues as necessary ('What he always says then is . . .', 'Now she would make an excuse and leave the room . . .', and so on). Do not worry about acting ability. Dive straight in as artificially as you like and the role play will soon come alive because these are live issues for you.

Use the guidelines on p. 53 to remind you of your priorities.

When you finish the role play talk with your partner or group about how it felt. Talk about what the difficult moments were for you, and also what the good moments were when you felt the argument swing your way, or you sense that your assertive stance was gradually removing obstacles to the outcome you felt was best in that situation. Use the guidelines on p. 54 to review your role-play exercise.

GUIDELINES FOR ROLE-PLAYING

1 **State your goal**
Specify the change you want in your own or the other person's behaviour.
Ask: 'What am I trying to achieve?'
'Is it solving the problem?'
'Is it realistic?'
'What is my fallback position?'

2 **Look at the possible strategies**
Evaluate by asking:
'If I say this, how is the other person likely to react?'
When?
Where?
How?

3 **Select optimum strategy**

4 **Suggested tactics**
(a)   Describe the problem to the other person.
(b)   Say how you feel by using 'I' messages and *owning the situation or problem*:
'I feel . . .'
'I think . . .'
(c)   Say what you want:
'I want . . .'
'I would like . . .'
(d)   Show you hear and understand by using empathy:
'I can see you are . . .'
'I can understand . . .'
(e)   Negotiate for a workable compromise by giving to get:
'If I give X, will you give Y?'
'This is what I want. If I give this, what are you prepared to offer?'
(f)   Use consistent body language.

REVIEWING ASSERTIVE BEHAVIOUR

Instruction: After role play, each person should answer the appropriate set of questions then compare answers with their partners.

If you were the assertive person:

1 Did you say what you wanted to say?
2 Were you direct and *not* apologetic?
3 Did you let the other person know how you felt?
4 Did you tell the other person what you wanted?
5 Did you let the other person know you understood and were listening to their point of view?
6 Now that you have asserted, how do you feel about yourself?

If you were a partner:

1 Did your partner stand up for their rights without infringing upon yours?
2 Did your partner stand or sit in an assertive position while speaking to you?
3 Did you feel they meant what they said?
4 Was your partner's voice relaxed, calm and strong?
5 Were your partner's gestures and body language appropriate to their message?
6 Now that your partner has asserted him/herself, how do you feel towards them?

If you were an observer:

1 Did the volume and tone of voice match what was being said by the assertive person?
2 In your opinion did they move on and reach a compromise?
   If not – can you suggest one?
3 Did the assertive person show they understood and use 'I' messages?
4 Please specify any other improvements to the assertive person.

STEP 11: IDENTIFYING A SPEAKING PARTNER

If you are in the process of becoming an assertive manager, a speaking partner will be very useful to you. You need:

- someone to share your emotional reactions with

- someone to discuss your ongoing problems with

- someone to commiserate with you on your failures

- and someone to enjoy sharing your successes with

Particularly when you first start to use it, assertiveness involves containing more emotion than usual. You don't have aggressive outbursts, you don't slam doors and sigh sighs, and you don't flop around passively. You are taking an assertive, active, adult and responsible role, far more than in the past. You need someone to let those emotions out with – someone who can empathise and understand.

After a few weeks or months, assertiveness actually makes it easier to express your true feelings because you learn ways of expressing strong feelings without losing control or starting a row: so it tends to be in the initial stages that you need support on the emotional front.

It is valuable to have an empathetic partner who can help you to analyse situations or relationships where you want to be assertive but feel blocked at the moment.

Sometimes you will try to be assertive and make a mess of it. You need someone to talk, commiserate, laugh, review and re-plan about it with.

Last but not least, you need someone to share your assertive successes with!

The ideal speaking partner is someone who understands your job but is in a different field from you (so that you are not in any future time going to find yourself in competition with one another) and who does not work in the same organisation as you (for similar reasons). It has to be someone whom you can trust, so that you can both feel clear that you will keep each other's confidence. They may be interested in having support with regard to assertiveness, or with some other aspect of their career development. The aim is to give each other good listening and support for an agreed amount of time (half an hour each, an hour each, whatever you've got time for) on a regular basis (once a week, once a fortnight, once a month) as planned together by the two of you.

It is a more formal arrangement than simply a meeting or a phone call between friends (although it may well take place within an already established friendship), and as such is a resource you can count on in your assertive development.

Sometimes there is nobody who could fulfil this role for you. When that is the case, consider keeping a journal in which you write about the day's or week's events in terms of your assertiveness and how it is developing, what impact it is having on your job and your colleagues and how you feel about it yourself. A journal is a good receptacle for feelings which, for the moment at least, you are not able to share with anyone else, and is a creative way to develop writing and analytic skills as well.

Having absorbed the basics of assertive technique, we can now move on to seeing their application in a variety of managerial contexts.

PERSONAL WORKSHOP REVIEW				
In this step	I was most surprised by	The most valuable point for me was	My action plan is	Any other notes
Step 1: Recognising 4 behaviours				
Step 2: Setting your own agenda				
Step 3: A Bill of Rights				
Step 4: Contact your strength				
Step 5: Active listening				
Step 6: Core phrase work				
Step 7: Personal style				
Step 8: Body and voice exercise				
Step 9: Breathing well				
Step 10: Assertiveness role play				
Step 11: Identifying a speaking partner				

PART II

Meetings   5

'Let me not to the marriage of true minds
Admit impediment . . .'

(Shakespeare, Sonnet 116)

How often are the meetings in your place of work the marriage
of true minds, or anything like it? All sorts of things go on at
meetings but it is disappointing how rarely there is a productive
and creative exchange of ideas leading to good collective
decisions. Nevertheless, use of assertive technique can facilitate
positive and productive meetings.

Many of the decisions which affect how you do your job, what
your future opportunities are going to be and what direction
your organisation as a whole is going to take are made at
meetings. If you are able to function well, powerfully and clearly
at meetings, then you can have a positive influence both on your
own prospects and on how the organisation itself develops.

We will look at the roles you may have to perform at meetings,
the types of meeting you may be engaged in, and some of the
problems you may encounter. They are:

- **Roles**
  Chairing
  Reporting
  Participating
  Representing

- **Types of meeting**
  Large
  One-to-one
  Project development
  Marketing
  Policy

- **Common problems**
  Interruptions
  Silent meeters
  Reaching closure on time

Assertiveness can be used to tackle each of these elements. (The trouble-shooting meeting is dealt with in Chapter 6, which discusses high-tension situations.)

ROLES

CHAIRING

'When I chair a meeting I feel my aim is *to be assertive on behalf of the task of the meeting.*'

If you bear this manager's formula in mind it becomes clear how to make the other decisions which arise in chairing a meeting. When someone is rambling on miles off the point, when should you intervene and bring them back to the agenda? When an argument arises which in your judgement is more of a personal sparring match than a debate useful to the meeting, when should you step in? When someone slaps a suggestion down without allowing due discussion, at what point do you ensure that discussion does take place?

The question to ask yourself is: 'What is necessary to be *assertive on behalf of the task of the meeting?*

Defining the task of the meeting

To manage this successfully you must know *what* the task of the meeting is, and this means that you must be properly prepared. Familiarise yourself with the agenda and read previously circularised papers. Deluged by printed matter, we all have to learn ways of reading that are not unlike the 'active listening' model of listening – that is, you learn to read very fast and summarise the main points for yourself as you go along.

Only if you have absorbed preparatory materials properly can you judge what the 'task of the meeting' is. In *Mind Your Manners*, John Mole comments dryly on the English tendency to regard such pre-meeting work as optional:

It is not usual for everyone to be well prepared. Even when papers are previously distributed they will not always be read. Lack of preparation does not inhibit passing of opinion and judgement.

This does not make a good impression on our international colleagues and competitors.

Control   A meeting brings together people with:

- information

- skills

- representative interests

- vision

You have to make sure all their data can be pooled and the best possible synthesis can take place. You will need to use the skills of 'contacting your strength', the core phrase and good prompting.

It takes confidence to be a good chair and have sufficient personal authority to keep the meeting on the rails. Use the 'contact your strength' skill (pp. 46–7) to help you feel strong and in control.

Contact your strength

In the heated and often claustrophobic atmosphere of meetings, the chair needs to work well on emotionally – and strategically – neutral core phrases to ensure that appropriate discussion takes place.

Utilise core phrases

Why do participants wander off the point at a meeting? They may want to impress other participants with their ideas and forcefulness. They may be feeling isolated in their work and use the arena of the meeting as a chance to communicate compulsively. They may be extremely concerned about something which does indeed need discussion but is not relevant to this particular meeting. Perhaps the most difficult person is the one who simply loves the sound of their own voice. When you are chairing it is useful to notice why a speaker is rambling, and adjust your core phrase accordingly:

'I can see you're very worried about X, John, but we can't deal with it at this meeting. Bring it up again at the Y meeting. What we must focus on here is . . .'

or

'I must stop you there. We must return to the point we are dealing with which is . . .'

The hooks you may get in return are:

'Let me just finish . . .' (manipulative)

'Don't you interrupt me . . .' (argumentative)

'Well I must say, no one's ever found it necessary to stop me in my tracks before . . .' (irrelevant logic)

Show you've heard (but not with too much empathy in case the other speaker gets the bit between their teeth again) and repeat your core phrase:

'No, we must move on. What we must focus on here is . . .'

'I understand that. We must return to the point we're dealing with, which is . . .'

An aggressive 'Don't interrupt me . . .' is difficult to deal with. Don't get into a 'yes you are/no I'm not' argument. Try:

'What I'm saying is that we must get back to the point, which is . . .'

Sometimes a determined wanderer-off-the-point will just go on talking right over the top of your interruption, as if wallpapering over you. Keep using your core phrase –

'I must ask you to stop there . . .'

and up the ante if you need to:

'I must stop you there.'

'Colin, I must stop you there.'

'There we must stop, and come back to our main point which is . . .'

Notice that using the person's name makes your assertive interruption more effective.

If you have to use repeated assertive interruptions like this, you must stay well grounded in good strong body language. You can allow your voice to become more authoritative as you reiterate your point if you want to but, except in the most exceptional circumstances, do not shout, even if the other person has begun to do so. It is much easier to keep control of the meeting if you hold on to your assertiveness and do not let it spill over into aggression.

Good prompting If members of the meeting have been slapped down or shut up by other domineering members, you may need to use your

assertiveness to draw ideas out of them. This must again be
done in a strategically – and emotionally – neutral way to
preserve the objectivity of the chair. Simply invite a contribution,
and ensure that the person has a fair chance to have their say:

'Janet – did you have a point to make on this?'

'Let's hear the suggestion Peter was in the process of making.'

'Alan, you were starting to explain something – could you
complete that explanation?'

MAKING A PRESENTATION

Presenting a report to a meeting can be nerve-wracking.
Important decisions may be made on the basis of the data which
you present. Your personal sense of authorship also makes you
feel vulnerable: if the report is rejected or rubbished, in a real
sense you feel rejected and rubbished too. Nevertheless,
presenting a report well is very satisfying, raises your personal
profile and may make a real contribution to your development
within the firm.

The skills of report-writing, and the use of all the visual aids
and design of materials, are an important part of any manager's
portfolio, and must of course be learned separately. The
assertive skills that come into play when presenting a report are
voice quality and body language.

Voice quality (see pp. 35–6)   Remember your basic formula
'lowish and slowish'. The most common mistake in presenting a
report is to rattle through, as though to get it over with. If your
report is well-structured and concise, you can afford to take it at
a steady momentum. Do not lose the force of what you are
saying by hurrying.

Low and slow

Sometimes you will present a report which is making a
strongly felt request, and sometimes you may need to present a
report which is highly critical of someone or something. In either
case, watch the voice timbre. Sounding pleading will not make
your case more persuasive, nor will sounding furious make your
evidence more damning. Stay within the assertive/resonant
range and the report really can 'speak for itself'.

Body language (see pp. 27–34)   Everybody is looking at you,
for at least part of the presentation, so the visual impression you
make is very important. Use the absolute body language basics:
lift your spine, drop your shoulders, keep the front of the body
long, keep the back of the neck long.

Stand tall and relaxed

Use the assertiveness principle of 'acting over' your emotions.
Maybe you do feel terrified – it does not have to show if you do

Control emotions

not want it to. It is an emotion you can share with your speaking partner later on. If you have practised assertiveness you have the specific skills to retain an appearance of calm and control, whatever is going on inside.

Make frequent eye contact

Sweep your gaze across all the faces in the room fairly frequently (at least every 2 or 3 minutes) so that you have at least some eye contact with all those present. Some people are far more receptive than others and will return your gaze and interact with what you are saying; some will always avoid your eyes. You must be politically alert here because, although it is tempting to address yourself mainly to any listeners who are nodding, smiling and receptive, it may look as though you are in some sort of private collusion with them. Be aware.

Control your hands

'What shall I do with my hands?' is the constant cry of anyone called upon to make presentations. If your hands seem to be a terrible liability,

(a) clasp them loosely behind your back or in front of you for most of the time,
(b) avoid fidgeting with them.

Once you have acquired competence in sticking to those two rules, you may find that you develop your own vocabulary of gesture which is expressive and individual, and not a liability at all.

Coping with catastrophes We have all been at or given presentations where disasters have happened. You fall over your own feet on the way to the flip chart, you drop your notes in a cascade which is then irretrievably out of order, you left the transparencies in the taxi, the electrics fuse: all the stuff of standard Freudian anxiety-dreams, and all things which can easily happen in real life.

Assertiveness is invaluable – you simply say what you feel, you negotiate for time if you need it, and you report on what you are going to do next: three core phrases one after another. It gives you a chance to 'act over' feeling panicky and flustered, and conversely, if necessary, it gives you a way of saying that you *are* flustered, while holding onto your dignity.

Should you be unlucky enough to fall over at a very public moment, console yourself that you are in the good company of Terry Wogan, Nancy Reagan and many many more public figures who have missed their footing with audiences of millions. Then take a moment to get your breath and work out whether you have hurt yourself. If you are not badly hurt just get up and brush yourself down. If you are good at instant witty remarks this is the time for one; if not, a short core phrase –

'Well, I don't seem to have hurt myself – so I'll continue with the presentation now!'

– will do. There's no need to apologise.

Suppose you drop your notes, or leave vital material behind, or the audio-visual equipment doesn't work? Report assertively what has happened:

'I've just realised I've left the transparencies in the taxi.'

'The electricity supply is off, so we can't use the video.'

'As you can see, I've dropped my notes!'

Negotiate for time if you want it:

'I need five minutes now to collect my thoughts and decide how to do this without the slides/video/reorganise these notes.
Could I ask you to take a short coffee break/talk amongst yourselves/bear with me while I do this/have a few minutes' fresh air [whatever is most appropriate].'

Apologise assertively if it feels sensible to do so, but don't roll in the dirt:

'I do apologise for this hold-up.'

Then, report what you are going to do next:

'I shall circulate you all with the statistics on the transparencies tomorrow. I can summarise the position and go on to . . .'

'I'll give you a brief run-down of what is on that video and organise a screening of it next week. We can talk about the issues it raises for us . . .'

'Thanks for bearing with me. I have my data in order now and can continue . . .'

Sometimes, paradoxically, you appear to be more in control by acknowledging that you aren't. Depending on the context, it may be useful to say:

'I feel quite shocked now . . .'

or

'I've momentarily lost my thread because of that . . .'

but only do so if you are sure it is not giving power away. Otherwise save your personal commentary on your nightmare presentation for the ears of your speaking partner.

PARTICIPATING

As well as being required to chair meetings, most managers will also frequently attend meetings as participants. The point about good preparation (p. 60) applies to participants just as much as to the chair. You can be much more effective at a meeting for which you have briefed yourself well, and you are at far less risk of wasting the meeting's time with queries to which you would know the answers if you had read the advance papers.

Your **tasks as a participant** in a meeting are:

1   to contribute your data and expertise when it is relevant
2   to ask for clarification of obscure points
3   to challenge points you feel are incorrect
4   to monitor any subtexts of the meeting

The **assertive skills** you need are as follows:

Contact your strength

1 In order to contribute your own information and expertise, you need to remember the self-esteem work in 'contacting your strength' (pp. 46–7). This helps to reaffirm in your own mind that your skills are good and therefore your contribution is valuable. It helps to counteract anything being said directly or indirectly to undermine your credibility or your point of view.

Use a core phrase

Using a core phrase helps to say what you want to say clearly and plainly. It also gives you a solid nucleus of words to work with and defend if your contribution is attacked. Remember to

Don't get hooked

avoid getting hooked (pp. 36–9), but remember too that a meeting is or should be an arena for exchanging ideas, so that you must be prepared to take new ideas on board which may call for an adjustment in your position. Because of this, it is

Have a fallback position

important to work out your fallback position (pp. 39–40) before you get into the cut and thrust of the meeting itself.

Contribute only when necessary

Remember only to contribute to the meeting when it is relevant, and to keep your contributions concise. This makes a more powerful impact than holding the floor for a long time and risking boring or irritating the other members of the meeting.

Be brief

There is only one case for interjecting when it is not strictly necessary and that is when for strategic reasons it is important for your voice to be heard and registered at least once. If you need to speak out for this reason, limit yourself to one brief point.

2 and **3** In clarifying obscure points and challenging incorrect ones, the first assertive skill you need is once again the power-within confidence to make a point calmly which you know may be controversial or may offend at least one other person at the meeting.

Be confident

The second is to avoid padding (p. 25) and unnecessary apologies:

Avoid padding

'I'm sorry, could you just explain . . .'

Instead, make positive requests:

Be positive

'I don't fully understand X. Could you talk us through it?'

'Can you go over how you arrive at this figure please?'

'Could you explain what the reasoning is behind that third recommendation?'

When you want to make a challenge, again it is better to avoid,

'I'm sorry, that's not right.'

This sounds shrill and truculent, and not particularly authoritative.

You can state your challenge or disagreement positively from a mild degree right through to a strong one:

Choose appropriate strength of challenge

'I do disagree with you there, in fact . . .'

'I must disagree with you there. My information is . . .'

'I believe that's incorrect. In fact . . .'

'That is incorrect. What actually happened was . . .'

'I think you're quite wrong. I believe . . .'

'I must disagree in the strongest possible terms. My view is . . .'

Pitch in wherever you feel is appropriate, but leave some space to build up the strength of your challenge if you need to. Cecil B. De Mille may have been able to 'Start with an earthquake and build up to a climax', but most of us have to start fairly quietly and build up to an earthquake only if absolutely necessary!

4 Monitoring the subtext is an assertive way of knowing what is happening in your organisation and taking care of yourself and your staff. At most meetings there are obvious, surface, verbal transactions; but there is also a subtext of other transactions at the level of moods, alliances, coldnesses, hints and innuendoes. You may think of these as gamesmanship or one-up-manship or as 'what is really going on'.

Clear detached observance of these 'games' will give you the strong position of understanding the hidden agendas between the people who are meeting together – their likes and dislikes, their rivalries and hopes – and therefore a certain amount of foresight into what is likely to happen next, who is likely to support what sort of plans, and who is likely to move where in the staffing structure.

The assertive skill here is very like that explained as 'proxemics' (pp. 28–9), but at an emotional and power-broking level. To be assertive you need to know where you stand, and clearly observing the subtext when you are a participant in a meeting will help you to do that.

REPRESENTING

You may be sent to a meeting as a representative of a group. Your task in this case is *to be assertive on behalf of the views and needs of the group you represent.*

This needs all the assertive skills required by the ordinary participant. In addition you must:

- keep a clear distinction between your views as an individual and the views of the group you represent

- keep a clear distinction between comment and criticism directed at the group you represent and that directed at yourself as an individual.

Many people find it easier to be assertive on behalf of a group they represent than on their own behalf. This is similar to the phenomenon of people physically defending someone else where they would find it difficult to defend themselves. We are well programmed to use our energy for the benefit of others.

In order to represent the group with whose voice you are entrusted in the best possible way, **use the core phrase system**, **avoid hooks**, and **keep your body language and voice quality strong**.

One further point: one sometimes needs to be assertive in pointing out who one does *not* represent. A woman, a black person, a gay person, or a person with disabilities may be asked for comments as though they could represent the whole group.

'Well, what do women feel about this then?'

'Is this what the black people here want?'

and so on.

You can point out that you have no mandate or wish to speak as though you were a representative of the group to which you happen to belong; but you need not lose the opportunity to make a useful point.

'I can't speak for all the women here, but as an individual woman I hope . . .'

'Remember, I'm not an elected representative of gay staff. I myself find that . . .'

'Firstly, I'm one disabled person, not a representative for all disabled people; but, working here and being disabled, I think we should . . .'

'My own suggestion on this would be . . . but I don't speak for all the black workers in the firm.'

TYPES OF MEETING

Different types of meeting each have their own particular dynamics and requirements for assertiveness.

As John Garnett, former director of the Industrial Society, used to say, twelve is the upper limit for the size of a workable team:

'After all, the good Lord only had twelve, and one of those was a wrong 'un!'

Twelve seems to be the psychological limit for a comfortable sense of 'small group' identity. In a group of more than twelve we start to feel as though we are in a large rather than a small gathering.

The two chief requirements for the participant in a large meeting are to avoid being intimidated, and to project more extensively in a large group.

On not being intimidated   The by now familiar skills of **contacting your strength** (pp. 46–7) and **taking care of your body language** (p. 50) will help enormously in not getting intimidated.

It helps too to diffuse the status of a large group by disassociating people from their intimidating job titles. This chief executive, that finance director, those equity partners, were

LARGE MEETINGS

Don't be intimidated by a job title

not assigned those roles at birth by a higher power, they are simply human beings performing those roles for their organisations for the time being. If there could possibly be said to be up sides to events as dreadful as the two recessions of 1981 (the industrial recession) and 1991 (the service recession), one of them might be that we have been confronted with the temporality of industrial and corporate power. Because so many apparently strong organisations have gone to the wall, we can see, in a way that was not clear in the burgeoning 1970s, that *anyone* can lose their job and their power; *nobody*'s exalted role is fixed in the firmament.

We are all vulnerable

Another useful mental manoeuvre when you are confronted by a group of people who intimidate you is to visualise them in their pyjamas, or imagine what they looked like as small children. This helps you to see them without their smart clothes and sharp haircuts, and to glimpse their vulnerable side. In turn this makes you feel less vulnerable. Any group of people, however enormous, is composed of human beings who once were babies who cried to be cuddled and fed. Stay in touch with that and nobody can scare you all that much.

See the large size of the group as an asset. It is easier to raise interest and energy in a large group than a small one if you communicate well. Instead of feeling, 'There are thirty people here and I only know four of them and I can't open my mouth', think 'There are thirty lots of energy here I can take with me if I can get them on my side'.

Projecting   In a larger meeting it is necessary to be a bit louder, a bit firmer, a bit more formal than in a small meeting of four or five people. It is a bit like the difference between TV acting and theatre acting. The TV camera picks up every nuance of movement and expression; the microphone registers quiet speech, sighs, tiny sounds. Similarly, in a small meeting people can speak quietly and notice each other's expressions and gestures in detail.

On the stage, an actor must have a larger, more resonant voice, must make gesture and expression larger to have an effect, must be more stylised. Meeting with a large group you must make a similar shift to be effective. Enlarge your voice and gestures slightly and be more in your public, formal person than in your more individual private self.

ONE-TO-ONE MEETINGS

A manager often has to meet one-to-one with staff and with bosses. The more fraught of these occasions, such as disciplinary meetings and redundancy notices, are discussed in Chapter 6. Let us look here at the dynamics of one-to-one meetings and how assertiveness can improve their effectiveness.

If a one-to-one meeting between yourself and a staff member goes well, it can dramatically improve their commitment and loyalty, their sense of membership of your team and their motivation. If they feel you listened to them properly and worked with them respectfully and well, they are going to have a much clearer sense of the point and value of their work. If a one-to-one meeting between yourself and your boss goes well, this too has a beneficial effect. Your own identity and profile are enhanced, your ideas and achievements are registered clearly, and any input and suggestions from you gain weight as a consequence. You yourself will benefit from feeling you are part of a coherent effort.

The two key assertiveness skills in a one-to-one meeting are to keep it structured and to use active listening.

Keep it structured   To use a one-to-one meeting effectively, do not think of it as 'a chat', even if that is how it has been referred to:

'Come and have a chat with me about your budgets, will you?'

or

'Let's have a chat about the design for the new brochure shall we? Tomorrow at 10.00 OK?'

Chatting is a kind of verbal companionship – sparring or dancing or wool-gathering or stroking, whatever it happens to be. It may be creative, but it is creative in a spreading, seeping sort of way, and needs an informal unstructured setting to grow and develop well.

A good one-to-one meeting is more like knitting than wool-gathering – you have made something specific by the end of it. It is creative in a way that is more often appropriate in a corporate setting.

Thus you will get the most from a one-to-one meeting if you ask yourself what *your* goal in that meeting is. The skill of **identifying your goal** is inherent in the skill of forming the core phrase (pp. 25–7), and is specified in the role-play exercise in Chapter 4 which requires you to identify your goal at the very beginning of the exercise (p. 53). Keep the meeting structured, keep it active and dynamic, and keep it moving. Use **good core phrases** to make any points you want to make, and match them with **coherent body language**. If the other person in the meeting intimidates you for any reason, remember the guidelines on avoiding intimidation mentioned in the section on large meetings.

Active listening   Having made the point that it is not just 'a chat' there is nevertheless an opportunity at a one-to-one meeting to hear material that the other person would not necessarily disclose to a large session. If this might be useful to you, add to your basic active listening skills (pp. 22–4) the use of the 'waiting silence'.

Many of us are very embarrassed by pauses and silences, and rush to fill them with verbal junk rather than let them run their course. For an assertive manager, though, silence can function powerfully and well in two ways.

First, with practice, you will become progressively less afraid to pause while you work out your own core phrases. Far from making you seem hesitant, this actually gives your words tremendous weight, because they seem, and indeed are, carefully considered.

Second, in a one-to-one meeting, the other person often wants to say something which they feel ambivalent about sharing, whether for strategic or other reasons. If you make a receptive space for them they may be more ready to tell you whatever it is that is on their minds, and this may be very important information for you.

Create a receptive space

You can do this with specific prompts:

'Is there anything else you'd like to say about that before we move on?'

'I wonder if there's anything else we should consider about this?'

'Now, do you think we've covered all the ground on that one?'

– remembering not to rush on after you have made this opportunity, but to leave a gap for a few moments. Or, with practice, you can learn simply to leave receptive gaps in the proceedings, into which material can come from the other person.

Remember that anyone can use 'waiting silences', including the person you are meeting with. Choose assertively for yourself whether to take that opportunity to disclose material. Do not walk into a waiting silence feet first unless you do so out of positive and assertive choice.

The aim at a project development meeting is to be creative and develop some new vision, and then to attend to the nitty-gritty of how it should be carried out. Both elements are equally important, whether you are getting a new project off the ground or keeping an established project moving. You need both assertive visioning and assertive pragmatism.

Assertive visioning   Assertive visioning means:

- overcoming inertia and getting in touch with your creative energy

- valuing your own ideas, believing they are worthwhile

- valuing others' ideas, being receptive to them

- forming a good synthesis with the resources available

Much of the managerial role involves fulfilling targets and meeting criteria which are already set. This requires all the chairing/finishing/completing skills. Being innovative means activating a different part of yourself – a certain playfulness, an ability to think laterally, to visualise risks, to see how things could be different.

You might have plenty of ideas. If so, validate them from the basis of good self-esteem, and suggest them without apologetic or anxious padding, in a concise and assertive structure.

If you're being asked for creative input and feel pressurised because you have not got any, do not panic. Look to the part of your life where you are creative at the moment; except at our bleakest moments there is always one somewhere. You may be being creative in design and innovation in your garden or your house; you may be being creative in a friendship or a love affair, or in being a parent. You may be working on a sport or your fitness generally, which is certainly a creative thing to do. You may play an instrument or sing in a choir or have drafts of a novel hidden in a dark drawer on which you work when you get the chance.

The point I am making is simply this: there are not 'creative' people and 'non-creative' people – everyone is creating their own life and their own biography. We all produce highly creative material every night of our lives in our dreams. If you feel temporarily blocked about expressing your creativity in the workplace, do not worry. Take time to notice and appreciate how creative you are in other aspects of your life, and you will in time identify the creative part of yourself and be able to activate it at work when you need to.

PROJECT DEVELOPMENT MEETINGS

Get in touch with creative energy

Value your ideas

Value other people's ideas

Assertive visioning means being able to hear and value other people's ideas as well as your own. Remember the 'Bill of Rights' (p. 45), which contains

'Everyone has the right to be listened to.'

and

'Everyone has the right to be treated with respect.'

Listening well to other people's creative suggestions is essential. Do not write people off because you do not like them or they do not usually have much to say. Neither of those things precludes them having a brilliant idea this time.

Listening well to other ideas also means having good self-knowledge and an understanding of the ebb and flow of your own energies. It can be difficult to listen considerately when you are all fired up about your own thoughts. Nevertheless it should be attempted.

Form a good synthesis

If all the members of a project development meeting contribute what they can and listen properly to each other, they should be able to come up with a realistic synthesis – a project that is workable within the resources available. This leads on to the next stage.

Assertive pragmatism   A marathon is 26 miles and 385 yards long. One runner said:

'The 26 miles are easy. It's the 385 yards that hurt.'

This applies to most substantial projects – so many lack that last bit of effort and determination to see them through to the very end.

Assertive pragmatism means:

- keeping the energy of the meeting going for practical decisions

- persisting assertively to tie up loose ends

- running the last 385 yards

These are your completer/finisher skills in action.

Ensure setting up of practical planning

It is no good having a wonderful vision if you do not assign roles and tasks to the staff, have target dates, deadlines and a reporting and monitoring system in place to ensure that everything is going according to plan. There is almost always a dip in the energy of a meeting when a vision has been agreed, and a tendency to rush the assignment of rules and the setting up of practical planning. You can use your assertive skills to make sure these are agreed quickly and clearly.

Use the 'repeat core phrase' technique to persist in tying up any loose ends. You can insist that details are finalised, without being heavy-handed, by avoiding getting hooked and staying with your core phrase:

Tie up loose ends

> 'I know you've got another meeting, but before you go, let's agree a date for the first progress report.'

> 'I see you're desperate for a cup of coffee, there are just two more jobs that need assigning first.'

> 'I understand you feel it's unnecessary to go into such detail now, but I am sure if everyone is clear what they have to do, we have a much better chance of success. Let's give it five more minutes now to get it right.'

Bear in mind that you need some extra push in nearly every project to see it through to its conclusion. An ability to 'run the last 385 yards' can make you an outstanding manager.

Run the last 385 yards

At a marketing meeting where you are selling, you must make good use of your assertive skills.

MARKETING MEETINGS

Your **personal style** (pp. 33–4) as a visual message makes the first impression on the client. Look for a sensitive balance between what you feel confident and strong wearing, and what the client will be comfortable with.

It is essential to be well **prepared** and well **equipped**. If you do your background research well and can answer most of the client's questions without hesitation, neither you nor he or she will mind if you occasionally have to say:

> 'I can't answer that at this moment. I'll make a note and get the answer to you tonight/tomorrow/next week [whatever is appropriate].'

Active listening is a key skill in marketing. Remember the aphorism doctors (the new generation anyway) are taught:

> 'Listen to the patient. He is telling you the diagnosis.'

Listen to the client: they are telling you what they will buy. This is not necessarily what they plan to buy or what they think at this moment they might buy. Listen carefully 'between the lines' and you will hear what they will buy.

Use your active listening and your awareness of body language to gauge when the client has 'had enough' – and go for a closure then: at best, a deal; otherwise, an arrangement for another contact and follow-up. Good selling means knowing when to leave well alone as well as knowing when to persist: providing good information and an excellent follow-up service may well do more business in the end than an immediate hard sell that makes the client feel pressurised. The ability to observe and 'read' other people that comes with practising assertiveness will help you know when to do which.

POLICY MEETINGS

Use of 'I' statements

Any meeting which decides policy, whether formally titled thus or not, sets the framework within which everything else in the organisation happens. Feelings inevitably run high at times.

Because of the serious implications of anything voted in a policy meeting, you must be prepared to use the strongest level of assertiveness to state your case. Be prepared to preface your core phrases with introductions like:

'I feel very strongly about this and I want to say . . .'

'I want to say that I absolutely disagree with the last speaker because . . .'

'I must make it quite clear that . . .'

'Let us have no misunderstandings about this. The point I want to make is . . .'

Concise introductory phrases like these add weight and urgency to what you say without detracting from your steady, assertive tone and stance. As such, they add to your authority and stature. They are an application of the part of the role-play exercise in Chapter 4 that suggests making an 'I' statement to express strong feelings (see Step 10, p. 52).

Just about all the items described in the other types of meetings can occur at a major policy-making meeting too. You may have to represent and defend the interests of your own team. You may have to take responsibility for contributing innovative suggestions, and responsibility for discussing how they should be carried out. You may have to take care of any tendency you have to feel intimidated, and to make sure you plug into your own self-confidence before you let your voice be heard. A broad spectrum of assertiveness skills, then, is of great value to you whenever you attend a policy meeting.

COMMON PROBLEMS

At the beginning of the chapter we identified three common problems arising at meetings: interruptions, 'silent meeters' and reaching closure on time.

When you are speaking in a competitive situation like a lively or aggressive meeting, you are going to get interrupted. What you need to know is how to re-interrupt so that you are sure to get enough of the time of the meeting to say what you need to say.

Essentially, this involves not getting hooked into the line of discussion initiated by your interruptor. You need not show any empathy in this circumstance, but do a bit of 'playback' (see pp. 37–8) and make a link back, however tenuous, into the material you want discussed. Avoid indirect aggression.

It's very easy to slip into sarcasm:

> 'Well I'm sure we are all fascinated by your plans, but shouldn't we really be concentrating on . . .'

This only succeeds in making you sound petulant. It also makes you enemies. Nobody likes being humiliated like that and they may form a conscious or unconscious plan to get their own back when they can.

Show you were listening, but without taking up the thread and getting hooked:

> 'That is important of course. Before we go into it I'd like to clear up those last few points on . . .'

> 'That's an interesting point. Nevertheless, can we focus for moment on . . .'

> 'I do agree we should come back to that later. I think we should get this sorted out first though . . .'

If you don't regain the initiative with your first re-interruption you might decide to try again, increasing the pressure as you feel is appropriate:

> 'That's obviously important, yes. Can I ask you to hold on while we reach a decision about X though?'

> 'I see you want to get that point across. I do think it's urgent that this meeting comes to a decision on X today though.'

> 'Yes, I take your point. On the other hand, I do strongly feel we should concentrate on and settle Y before we go on to anything else.'

INTERRUPTIONS

Don't get 'hooked'

If you don't prevail the second time, take stock and decide whether to back off and come back at a later point in the meeting. That may feel more advantageous. If that is your decision, relax, do not seethe and come back clearly with your core phrases when you gauge the moment is right.

If you decide you really must get the floor again immediately, go up one more gear:

'Madam Chair, I must ask the meeting to concentrate on X and not get sidetracked. We must get a decision on . . .'

'I must insist that we do not go off in another direction until we have cleared up Y . . .'

'It's urgent that we get back to the essential point here, and that is . . .'

'There is no time to waste here, and I regard this as a waste of time. I think it's vital that we get Y finalised.'

The last quotation is a good example of the use of assertive anger. The speaker expresses strong feelings using an 'I' statement, thereby avoiding an 'Oh yes it is/Oh not it isn't' argument. So long as the tone remains level, even though the statement is strong, it will come over as authoritative, assertive, demanding of attention and forceful, without being aggressive.

Taking up more space

A particular piece of body language which may be useful to you if you want to re-interrupt, and which is also applicable any time you want to take more control, is 'taking up more space'. This technique originates in martial arts and self-defence disciplines.

You can 'take up more space' in any position – standing or sitting, it does not matter. Simply:

1 steady your breathing, as in the breathing work (Step 9 in Chapter 4),
2 visualise energy radiating out around you like an all-over halo.

The effect of doing this is to relax and extend your body and your personality. People literally appear to expand when they do it: they seem to be taking up more space. As well as assisting in re-interrupting at difficult meetings, I find this a good way of getting served in a crowded bar!

SILENT MEETERS

Every organisation has its silent meeters. Maybe you are sometimes one yourself. The silent meeter is very disruptive because he or she sits through the meeting without making any contribution or expressing any views and then goes back to their own team without any of their questions answered, or any of their negative reactions sorted out. The chances are that they will complain among colleagues and give negative feedback about the meeting, its participants and the decisions it came to.

How do you 'bring out' the Silent Meeter? Active listening is essential once they do start to talk, but assertive prompting is the technique to start them off.

The core phrase you choose for prompting will vary according to precisely what message you want to convey. At its most straightforward it could be:

Assertive prompting

'It would be useful to hear your comment on this.'

You might want to register the fact that you have noticed their behaviour before:

'There have been difficulties in the past when we have not had input on this and then there have been complaints and problems later. Can you tell us now how you think this will work out for you and your colleagues?'

You might want to make some affirmative encouragement:

'It would be very helpful at this point to hear your views.'

Make a point of rounding up agreement or making a space for objections:

Make space for comments

'Can we take it that there are no problems with this?'

'Has everybody said everything they want to about this?'

There can then be no possible excuse for complaints and disruptive grumbling later, or for projects to stall because of a poor flow of communication by the Silent Meeter.

REACHING CLOSURE ON TIME

The energy of an organisation is badly dissipated when all that happens at meetings is that more meetings are set up, so all participants really need to work towards concrete decisions on agenda items wherever possible.

Ideally the chair takes responsibility for pacing a meeting so that it is possible to get through the agenda on time. If the chair is not active enough about this, other members of the meeting will have to move the pace on so that the agenda is satisfactorily covered.

Assertive prompts

Use assertive prompts –

'We're moving into the final half an hour of this, so let's keep everything as concise as we can.'

'There's about 10 minutes to go now. Can we briefly cover . . .'

'I see we're nearly out of time and I'd very much like to get this agreed . . .'

– to tie up as many loose ends as you feel it useful to finalise.

Assertive interruption

Remember your assertiveness skills if you need to interrupt:

'We must keep it brief at this stage. Do go on, but be as concise as you can.'

and assertiveness can be useful from the chair,

'I see there are 20 minutes left. Let's aim to get through to item 8 in that time.'

All the assertive skills mentioned in this chapter – from establishing your own self-confidence to being capable of speeding up or prompting other people assertively – can be used to ensure that there is an optimum outcome. It is important to be assertive about making and validating your own contribution, listening to and reviewing other people's input, and being as aware as possible of the dynamics of the meeting. This will enable you to influence the meeting within the time-frame you have got, towards an outcome (or a series of outcomes) which is good for the organisation and good for you.

Management at High Tension 6

*W*E all fear certain aspects of management. We cringe at the prospect of dealing with embarrassing issues, and shudder at the thought of giving bad news. It may at times be necessary to be extremely angry. Most of us dread this, and equally dread dealing with anger from others.

This chapter is concerned with using assertiveness to cope with transactions of high tension. We will look at the following heart-sinking necessities:

- saying 'no'

- dealing with embarrassing personal issues

- supporting staff with disciplinary matters and complaints

- righteous anger – necessary confrontations

- defusing anger – managing an angry onslaught

- coping with violence

- making staff redundant

There are ways of dealing with such situations which can leave you feeling more positive.

SAYING 'NO'

However flexible and responsive you try to be, from time to time you have to say 'no' – to your own staff, to clients, and indeed to your boss. It is essential in all these cases to be able to say a clear, powerful and assertive 'no'.

The inhibitions about making refusals come from anxieties:

- What will the other person feel?

- What will the consequence be?

- Will the refusal be taken seriously?

WHAT WILL THE OTHER PERSON FEEL?

'When you say "no" you are refusing the request, *not* rejecting the person.'

This formula helps to deal with the anxiety 'what will the other person feel?'

The fear, and to some extent the programming, is to believe that people will take a refusal as a personal rejection. But this need not be the case. Your own firm assertiveness can take 50 per cent of the responsibility for making it an adult–adult transaction. The other 50 per cent must be taken by the other person. Only by avoiding excessive 'parenting' of the other person can a real assertive exchange be established. Part of the skill is to learn to leave the other adult in the transaction to do their 50 percent. As an assertive manager you can be a good role model for giving and receiving assertive refusals.

WHAT WILL THE CONSEQUENCE BE?

Worrying about the consequences of saying 'no' is to do with three things:

- making a mistake

- making an enemy

- myth and magic

Making a mistake Perhaps you *are* wrong. Perhaps in turning down this suggestion, that project, the other initiative, you are making a radical mistake. Well, maybe so, and all managers have made decisions, both positive and negative, which they have lived to regret. However, you have made the best-considered decision that you can, on the basis of data and instinct. Now, you have to let it go. Review it later, alter it later, regret it later, whatever is necessary, but for the moment simply accept what you have done and let it go.

Making an enemy   If your workplace is full of people who believe 'don't get mad, get even', you may be concerned that you will make an enemy when you make a refusal. Strong assertive behaviour is essential in an aggressive atmosphere. Being intimidated is not a good reason for saying 'yes' instead of 'no'. Your calm and self-respecting attitude will help you stand your ground during the encounter itself, and an overall awareness of the internal politics of your organisation can keep you aware of the 'getting even' factor, if it is going to arise.

Myth and magic   A sense of myth and magic occurs within us because of experiences we had when we were very young. In the case of making clear refusals, it may be more powerful for women than for men. (It is not that men are immune to myth and magic, but that, culturally, they are more likely to experience them in relation to, for example, the sort of car they drive, or their sporting prowess or lack of it.)

It is irrational to feel that disaster may strike if you say 'no' to anything, and it reflects a cultural conditioning, particularly of women, to be complaisant and cooperative at almost all costs. If it feels really dangerous to you at an emotional level, regardless of practicalities, to say 'no', you are probably dealing with that childhood imperative. Some men and many women also feel a fear of becoming angry because it seems dangerous at an emotional level, regardless of practicalities. This is due to the same thing – a childhood experience of it being very dangerous to be angry.

Patterns which were laid down in childhood cannot be dismantled all in a moment. However, we can begin to re-examine them and change them gradually.

WILL THE REFUSAL BE TAKEN SERIOUSLY?

What if the other person just carries on doing what you asked them not to? What if they behave as though you agreed to their proposal?

Such a situation is basically a case of 'not getting hooked'. It is highly provocative to continue with a course of action when someone has refused permission, or agreement or support for that action. You will notice that in an immediate rise in your own tension if your refusal has been overridden or ignored. Show you see what has happened, and repeat your core phrase.

'I've received the brief for project [playback] even though I made it clear that I do not want to be involved [repeats core phrase]. I'd like to repeat again that I don't feel it is sensible for me to take that on, for the reasons I explained at our meeting [further repetition of core phrase].'

Report strong feelings with an 'I' statement if it is necessary:

'**I'm amazed to see** [reports strong feelings] that you took this action with client Y [playback]. I specifically asked you not to when we spoke [repeats core phrase]. You must stay within the boundaries we agree in future [additional core phrase].'

'My name is on the list of speakers for this seminar when I clearly said I was not available [playback]. You will have to change the programme, because I am not available on that date [repeats core phrase]. I feel very angry about this [reports strong feelings].'

Anyone ignoring your refusal is, consciously or unconsciously, overtly or implicitly, challenging your personal authority, whatever your job title is. Contact your strength, and stand your ground!

SAYING A CLEAR 'NO'

To say a good, clear 'no' remember these guidelines:

- pay attention to your immediate physical reaction, and trust it

- don't pad

- don't apologise

- don't hang around

The heartsink sign

Pay attention to your body   Your immediate physical reaction to a request is a very good indicator of how you *want* to respond. Your heart will clearly sink if you want to say 'no'. Your body will feel lighter and more elated if you want to say 'yes'. Trust these reactions. They give you a true picture of what you want, and that is something you need to know.

You may have to override that want, for practical, strategic or other reasons. It is still useful for you to notice what your immediate physical reaction was.

Don't pad and don't apologise   When you say 'no' you do not have to explain why or to apologise unless

(a)   you want to,

or

(b)   it is professionally necessary to do so.

You have a choice. You have the right to say no without explaining, if that is what you need to do at that time. You only have to explain if you feel you want to, or if you feel it is part of your job. Avoid saying 'sorry' unless you mean it. Use neutral introductory words or phrases like 'Unfortunately . . .' or 'The answer on this occasion is . . .' or 'I've thought this over carefully and . . .' Do not apologise as you introduce your explanation. Use a phrase like, 'My reasons are . . .' or 'The thinking behind the decision is . . .'

Don't hang around   When you have said what you need to say, go. Get off the phone, or leave the room, or change the subject completely. If you hang around, the risk is that you will start to say things like:

'Will that be OK, will you manage?'

'Look, I'm sorry to disappoint you . . .'

'I hope you're not going to take this personally . . .'

'I know you think I'm unreasonable, but you'll realise in the long term . . .'

All such comments undermine your assertive 'no'. They allow the other person to start wondering – Did you really mean it? Could you still be persuaded? Can you be manipulated via your obvious sense of discomfort and guilt? They give all your power away.

If the person who has received the 'no' has a strong reaction, they must take responsibility for dealing with that reaction themselves; and you must let them do so. If you can follow a 'no' with an assertive positive suggestion –

'No, you can't do X, but would you like to consider doing Y?'

– obviously it is helpful, but it is not always possible.

Letting the conversation trail off into unclear boundaries does not help either of you. Stay committed to your 'no' and go away!

EMBARRASSING PERSONAL ISSUES

From time to time in your career as a manager you will, without doubt, have to confront people about embarrassing personal issues. Naturally one wants to avoid it, hoping it will sort itself out. However, it often doesn't, and the embarrassing issue eventually has to be faced. How can assertive technique help when that happens? We will take as examples four particularly embarrassing areas: body odour, sexual behaviour, excess drinking, and personality clashes.

BODY ODOUR

Body odour is such an intimate subject that we all dread having to talk to employees or colleagues about the fact that their co-workers dislike their smell. However, sometimes it has to be done.

First, at the risk of conjuring up the ludicrous picture of managers covertly sniffing around their staff, it is worth getting clear that there are a range of personal smells that are linked with how we eat and how we live.

A meat-eating Northern European who uses salt and pepper, and maybe drinks beer and smokes cigarettes, will have different odours in their sweat from a Southern European who eats food containing plenty of garlic and drinks chiefly wine, or an Asian person who eats food spiced with curry and drinks tea. A teetotal vegetarian's sweat will smell different from that of a person who follows a macrobiotic diet or of someone who eats mainly fried foods. Someone who jogs or rides a bike to work smells different from someone who travels in on a crowded commuter train, and different again from someone who walks in through the park or drives in in a car and smokes cigarettes as they do so.

Lots of different kinds of sweat smells are perfectly acceptable, and one should be sensitive to complaints about smells which are really intolerance of a different life style or a different culture. What is offensive to just about everybody is stale sweat, of whatever kind, and if that is complained about one has to respond.

A personal training officer speaks about the consequences of failing to deal with this issue assertively.

'A woman employee who was very keen to develop her career regularly came on in-house training courses. She smelled quite strongly of stale sweat, a smell which was exacerbated whenever she did work which made her nervous and caused her to sweat more. It was particularly bad on a presentation skills session when all the delegates were videoed. They all found that nerve-wracking, but this woman really began to smell terrible. People were fairly unsubtle about opening windows and it was noticeable that other delegates were avoiding working with her on the pair-work exercises.

I wish I had had the guts to talk to her after the first course she came on, and failing that I should certainly have said something after the presentation skills course.

I still haven't done anything about it because I am so afraid of hurting her feelings and I am so embarrassed. The result of doing nothing is that when staff ring to apply for places on courses they sometimes actually ask me if she will be there, and ask to be put in a different group from her if she is. So I end up colluding in what is really very unpleasant gossip and not dealing with the situation at all.'

A manager in a similar department *did* manage to speak out about offensive smell, perhaps because it was one of his own staff of trainers who was causing offence. Because a staff member was fast becoming known as someone unpleasant to work with simply because of his body odour, this was clearly prejudicing the manager's ability to deliver the service he was meant to provide.

The manager in this case says:

'I knew I had to do something and I decided just to be direct. I said "A number of people have complained to me that they're bothered by your body odour. Can you sort it out?" He took it pretty well, just said "OK, thanks for telling me, I'll do something about it." And that was that. Mind you, I'd have found it far more difficult to say that to a woman.'

Assertive and sensitive

And one does have to be aware of gender issues in the area of embarrassing personal material, and to be prepared to delegate the matter to someone of the same sex as the person presenting with the problem, if that seems more appropriate.

If it is useful to do so, use the 'I' statement rule, and name the discomfort in the atmosphere – this will defuse it somewhat:

'I find this embarrassing but there's something we must discuss . . .'

or

'This is embarrassing for both of us: come on, let's face up to it and sort it out . . .'

SEXUAL BEHAVIOUR

The whole area of sexual behaviour is deeply personal and complicated by the fact that none of us is without hang-ups and histories of our own which affect our judgement. Most people would concur that, unless it is criminal, a person's sexual behaviour is his or her own affair and is of concern to their manager only if it is having a detrimental effect on their own or anyone else's work. The difficulties, of course, come in deciding when that boundary is crossed. What you can do is be responsive and empathetic to any problems your staff do bring to you, and be calm and assertive in your responses.

Be clear why it's your business

The issue of sexual harassment in the workplace is dealt with in Chapter 9. We will concentrate here on the way sexual behaviour can impact on the working team.

One senior manager describes how a love affair between two junior managers, both of them married to other people and one of them with a young family, had changed from something he privately disapproved of but felt was none of his business, into something where he felt he had to comment. The couple had been discreet for a number of months, but then started taking time out of the office in the afternoons, more or less simultaneously, and on more or less equally flimsy pretexts. At this point the junior staff became very intrigued and rather disturbed by the whole thing.

The senior manager spoke with each of them separately and requested assertively that they organise their relationship more discreetly again. Embarrassing though this was for all three of them, it did resolve the negative effect that the relationship was having on the output of the firm. His core phrase was along the lines of:

'Your private life is none of my business unless it affects things at work, but it becomes my business when it does. I want you to make sure you organise your relationship in such a way that it does not disrupt the junior staff, or distract other people from what they're getting on with. Do be sure that absences from the office in working hours are strictly related to work too.'

Inappropriate sexual relationships between professionals and their clients are another source of tension. Women are beginning to find the courage to confront the unethical sexual advances made by doctors, lawyers, therapists and other professional advisers. Less often, an unsuitable and unethical link is made across the genders the other way around.

The manager of a team of psychiatric social workers became concerned that a woman in his team was having a sexual relationship with a client. Such a relationship would be professionally off-limits. He takes up the story:

'I had to confront a staff member about making her relationship with a resident too special (I was suspicious of a sexual relationship in the background). This made me very tense in anticipation, but it seems that a good preparatory technique is a sleepless night, as after hours of rather wild and chaotic thinking (made wilder by my fury at being unable to sleep), I went to work and pulled it off with such crispness and clarity and so little flummery that I was barely recognisable and shocked the staff member concerned to the core with my cold brevity.

I think that such situations as being suspicious (and possibly having a disciplinary hearing in the offing) do require assertiveness in managers. The temptation is to play it low-key, because it's less embarrassing if the suspicions are ill-founded. I felt on this occasion that my dramatic change of style was a good thing. It redefined boundaries that were becoming confused. If I'd pussy-footed around and been duped I'd have felt guilty if later on it came to light that she had been having this affair. Having been direct I shan't feel guilty if it turns out I was right, as she will be the guilty one for having lied. If I was wrong, I simply asked a direct question and got a direct answer.'

The sleepless night, while doubtless infuriating at the time, probably was useful in this case because it allowed this manager to work through all the ifs, buts, hooks and pitfalls before the scene took place. When it did, he was free of all that, and the exchange was completely clean and clear.

As he says, whatever the eventual outcome, he now feels greatly relieved at having effectively done his job in protecting the client, establishing the professional disciplinary boundaries, and being direct and honest with his team member on this sensitive subject.

Relief once the air is clear

EXCESSIVE DRINKING

Many corporate cultures have an ambiguous relationship with alcohol. While afternoon inebriation might be completely unacceptable in blue-collar workers and dangerous for anyone operating machinery, and out of the question for anyone dealing face to face with members of the public, it's often rather benignly regarded in the executive tier. Drinking together, commiseration over hangovers and competing over how much was drunk when may be important ingredients of the culture and corporate bonding.

What does your company think about drink?

In this context it becomes difficult to discuss with anyone the fact that you feel they are drinking too heavily. As with the questions of sex and sexuality, it would seem that the crossover from 'their own business' to 'your business' comes when their behaviour starts to have an adverse effect on 'the business'.

The assertive core phrase, backed by coherent body language, is ideal for coping with a tricky situation like this:

'It's not acceptable to arrive back at the office in the afternoons and not be able to function to a good professional standard. You need to cut down on lunchtime drinking.'

It's vital, particularly in a context where bravado about drinking is admired, to keep your face relaxed and not contorted into a placatory grin, and to avoid slipping into an apologetic tone. If you feel embarrassed, say so:

'I feel awkward saying this – but it's important so it's got to be said. It's not acceptable . . .'

You may need to field several hooks:

'Who says my work isn't up to scratch in the afternoons?'

'You're not averse to a drink yourself, I'd say you've got a nerve to pull this on me.'

'What is this, a nursery school? Don't tell me what I can and can't do in my own time.'

Show you've heard, make a short reply if necessary, and repeat your core phrase:

'I have felt for some time that your work is below par in the afternoons and I'd like you to set a lower limit for the amount you drink at lunchtime.'

'Yes I do sometimes have a drink over lunch, but I set clear limits on it. Your work has deteriorated in the afternoons, and I'd like you to cut down on your lunchtime drinking.'

'Yes you can do what you prefer in your own time. My concern is with what you do here. Your work in the afternoons is not satisfactory and I'd like you to cut back on the amount you drink at lunchtime.'

Having dealt with aggressive hooks, if you sense the person him/herself is concerned about their use of alcohol, you can offer some support:

'Do you feel as though your drinking is getting out of hand? If you do, maybe we can do X and Y about it?'

Passive hooks can be difficult to manage too:

'I'm having such a bloody awful time at work at the moment and things are not good at home either. I need that drink to get me through the afternoon.'

Show empathy and repeat the core phrase:

'I'm sorry to hear things are so difficult for you, but your work has gone downhill in the afternoons, and I'd like you to limit the amount you drink at lunchtimes.'

Once you have got your point across, you can, again, offer some support:

'Is there anything we can do to help you find a more constructive way of coping with your difficulties?'

Once the person you're speaking with has taken in clearly both what you are saying and the fact that you mean it and want some action, end the interview with a fairly low-key but still assertive closure such as,

'I'll leave that with you then.'

Don't hang around and don't allow them to hang around – get yourself or them on to the next activity. When you're asking someone to take in something that they may find shocking or upsetting, so long as you've been clear and direct with them the most productive thing to have next is a pause during which they can reflect.

A manager may have to deal with conflicts between members of her or his staff, and both confront the situation and remain impartial while it is sorted out. A consultant describes the damage that can be done if this is not done properly:

MANAGING PERSONALITY CLASHES

'At a firm I was called into there was a dreadful personality clash between two managers. This had turned into a rift which led the whole company to be split down the middle – you were either one of X's people or one of Y's. The senior managers and directors just turned their backs on it really. They found it so difficult that they avoided thinking about tackling it altogether. I think they should have made the two of them work some sort of modus vivendi out. What eventually happened was that X went straight to the MD and said either Y goes or I go, and he swung it, which shocked and undermined everybody. It wasn't good practice, and staff morale was certainly lowered throughout the company.'

A long-term solution

You would need an extended strategy to cope with this tense scenario: perhaps separate meetings with each of the people concerned to hear their points of view, and to put the assertive message across that the overt hostility between the two of them is not acceptable and must be resolved professionally and sensibly; followed by a short series of meetings between the two of them together aimed at finding working solutions or truce agreements on their major differences; followed by a three- or six-monthly review and, ideally, as soon as practical and appropriate, involving them in a joint project together. Such a long-term view would be clear in your mind as you dealt with each encounter.

Typically, managing this would involve dealing with a lot of hooks of the type of:

'He's quite impossible. He just doesn't talk sense at all.'

'She's completely unreasonable. Don't ask me to waste my time with a person like that.'

A strong assertive line is necessary:

'My response to what you're saying is that the overt hostility between the two of you has got to stop, it isn't acceptable. Our meeting today is to work out how to manage that.'

It has to be clear that you will not be bullied, emotionally blackmailed or politically annexed by either of them.

SUPPORTING STAFF WITH DISCIPLINE AND COMPLAINTS

On disciplinary matters and customer-related issues, managers must give assertive support to their staff in the first instance. The manager of a bookshop says:

'I need to be assertive to customers who make complaints about staff, because I think that staff have a right to expect their manager to defend them in the first instance until proved guilty. I have to fight off the urge to be apologetic ad lib. I say things like, ''I'm sorry you were treated in such-and-such a way. I'm very surprised as the assistant concerned is usually very attentive (or whatever). But I'll certainly mention it to them."'

A supervisor of drivers expresses his exasperation when the opposite happens to him:

'I've got men on my staff on their third and fourth final warnings. Management just haven't got the bottle to sack anyone. It makes a mockery of the disciplinary procedures – they do what they want and more or less laugh in my face.'

A headmistress manages well both to hear the complaint of a parent with a child unhappy with his teacher, while supporting the teacher and gaining time to investigate the matter, by saying to the anxious parent,

'I'm sorry that Daniel's been so unhappy, but thank you for sharing that with me. I'll talk to Mrs C. after school today to see how she's been getting on with him and ring you later on to talk about it further.'

Putting it in writing   With someone who regularly wrong-foots you, or with an issue where you may want to go back over the history of it later, one of the assertive things you can do is to put it into writing.

'I wished to complain about something a manager in an organisation we're in partnership with had done, so I wrote rather than rang. This was a way of making the point emphatically, and putting it on record for the future. It meant too that I was clearly setting the agenda, which is by no means always the case when we talk.'

When you write you have as much time as you need to evolve your core phrase and avoid padding. Any hooks that come will be delayed, so you have time to anticipate them; but remember that they could arrive telephonically as well as by letter! If this happens you will have to transfer your skills to dealing with the matter 'live'.

RIGHTEOUS ANGER – NECESSARY CONFRONTATIONS

The manager of a local government department of archaeology had to undertake a visit to a sea-bed drilling rig which was drilling straight through a medieval waterfront without any reference to her or any regard for the regulations.

Set an achievable goal

Her realistic goal was to try to see whoever was in charge and put her objections, together with pointing out the breach of regulations. She doubted that she would be able actually to stop the drilling that was taking place, but felt that if she made her point clearly it would at least inhibit the rig being used again so blatantly in breach of the same rules. From the reaction to her telephone call in advance of her visit she anticipated a hostile reception. She decided to take a rather hefty male colleague with her for moral support. In spite of an intimidating atmosphere, a language problem which made communications even more fraught and the fact that she could not identify exactly who was in charge, she managed to make her point clearly and felt it *would* make a difference to where drilling was carried out in the future.

There was an implicit threat to her in that situation, but she dealt with it well by taking steps to ensure her physical safety, setting a realistic goal, and repeating her core phrase in spite of the difficulties.

MANAGING AN ANGRY ONSLAUGHT

A woman described how a client who had lost his temper leaped more quickly than she had been able to anticipate from their meeting table to a position between her and the door. As his shouting continued she recalls:

> 'I said to myself "Right, you're in a threatening situation, now relax" and deliberately did so. I then began to talk slowly to the client, keeping my voice steady, making no sudden movements, and saying, "Look, you're intimidating me, can you come and sit down and we can try to sort it out" and things like "I want to hear what you have to say, come and sit down. I can't understand you properly like this – sit down again and let's sort it out."'

By showing empathy, slowing down the pace and showing that she wanted a win–win solution, she gradually defused what was a dangerous loss of control on the part of her client.

An incident which I shared occurred at a motorway service station. I had just parked and was walking towards the restaurant across the car park when a hired minibus pulled in, a dozen or so men in their late 20s jumped out and began urinating against the van, two or three of them moving onto a grassy patch near my car and urinating there, with much yelling and leering, clearly intending to cause offence. The smell was horrible and I felt angry and threatened. The other customers in the car park used the standard British method of looking away and pretending it wasn't happening, especially the men, who clearly felt particularly threatened by this macho display.

I marched into the restaurant and requested to see the manager, having worked out my core phrase:

> 'There's a group of men peeing everywhere in the car park and I am feeling angry and threatened.'

The manager was a slight young man who reacted admirably in that he listened to what I was saying, thanked me for telling him, and said of course he would move these people along. He strode off immediately to the car park, with me scampering anxiously in his wake torn between wondering what marvellous leadership and self-defence skills he had been trained in and feeling astonished at how stupid he was in tackling a dozen heavily built and belligerent drunks on his own. I thought at least I could try to support him! If he knew any inspirational techniques though, I did not see them because by the time we reached the car park the offending group had gone. Nevertheless, I was most impressed by the way he handled my complaint, took in the information in it, took responsibility for it straight away, and acted on it. He clearly was prepared in his own mind to get the message, 'We don't want you here behaving like this', across and to deal with all the 'Who's going to make me?', 'You and whose army?' and similar hooks, as they arose, by remaining calm and authoritative.

COPING WITH VIOLENCE

Avoiding violence

The best way to cope with violence is to anticipate it and avoid it. If you feel an encounter may be dangerous, ensure if possible that you do not have to deal with it alone. If a client or colleague who you consider may be violent is visiting you in your office, leave the door open if possible while you meet, and organise the furniture so that you have a clear exit if necessary. Keep the temperature of the meeting very low and very slow, avoid any aggression at all on your own part, but stay grounded in your own strength. You have every right to decide what your own personal limit is in terms of physical danger, and, if you feel it is exceeded, to get straight out of the risky situation and get support.

Self-defence training

If physical attack is a possibility you may face, it could be an assertive decision to learn some physical self-defence. No course you attend and no book you read can make you invulnerable, but some basic knowledge can give you some extra options. *Her Wits About Her* is an excellent book of 'self-defence success stories' which describes the sense of self-worth and determination which inspires survival rather than becoming a victim.

Imaginative and empathetic people may be hesitant because they sense that anybody who becomes violent is deeply damaged inside themselves. You can in fact remain compassionate but still believe that it is right to protect your own body from assault. It is a fundamentally assertive action to defend yourself.

MAKING STAFF REDUNDANT

Of all the high-tension, high-temperature functions a manager may have, making staff redundant is probably the worst of all.

The whole process – from the decision that redundancies are necessary through selecting who has to go, to actually telling the people concerned, and explaining what has happened to remaining staff – is horrible from beginning to end and most people hate it.

Even someone who does not actually hate it and who prides themselves on seeing it in terms of economic necessity, will tend to find that the actual meeting in which they sack the member or members of staff *is* stressful, and the management of the emotional backlash among other members of staff is stressful too.

Making staff redundant assertively involves the following:

- giving the message that you are making them redundant clearly and without padding at the beginning of the interview

- dealing with the reaction

- giving a few clear reasons if appropriate

- giving clear and accurate information on the legal rights of the person concerned

- thinking ahead to escorting the person from the building if necessary

- telling remaining staff clearly what has happened and why

- recognising the strain on yourself and getting support for yourself after the event

When the time comes for the redundancy interview you will probably find yourself tense and nervous. Your obligation to yourself is to remain calm and keep your own boundaries as a professional; your obligation to the staff member is to be clear, accurate and calm with them.

The temptation of course is to beat about the bush and delay the moment of having to say 'You've lost your job'. This is passive behaviour and makes things worse for both of you.

Work out carefully what your core phrase is: at least this is an occasion where you *will* have time to work out that core material in advance. You may want to give a couple of reasons with your initial core phrase, but keep them short. It is far worse for your staff member to listen to a rambling lecture on the economy and your particular industry, wondering what is going on and dreading the worst, than to hear it directly:

> 'The recession has hit us hard and we can no longer avoid making staff cuts. I'm sorry to say I have asked you to this meeting to tell you that we are cutting your job.'

or,

> 'You have now had the required number of warnings and your work has not improved. This meeting today is to tell you that you have lost your job.'

Clearly one's emotions are different when sacking a valued and competent worker because of slump or takeover from when sacking someone whose unsatisfactory performance has been a drag on the firm for months. The risk in the first case is to become passive, because you regret what you are doing, and in the second case to become aggressive, because you feel this unpleasant situation is the other person's fault. It is important to try to remain assertive and balanced in either case.

Once you have given the clear message, the person involved may react in a number of different ways. She or he may be very angry, or burst into tears, or go into a kind of numb shock. They may of course behave in a dignified and assertive way.

If the reaction to that first clear message 'You have lost your job' is anger or tears, use the assertiveness technique described as 'not getting hooked' (see pp. 36–9).

GIVING THE MESSAGE

Stay calm

Prepare core phrases

Remain assertive

DEALING WITH THE REACTION

Don't get hooked

Show you see the other person's reaction,

'I see you're very angry about this . . .'

or

'I see you're very upset about this . . .'

If it's useful, repeat the core phrase or material:

'and we are facing the fact that you are losing your job here . . .'

'and we are dealing with the fact that we're making you redundant here.'

Then move firmly on to the next two stages.

GIVING REASONS (IF APPROPRIATE) AND OFFERING INFORMATION ON RIGHTS

Should the tears or the anger persist, you may need to use a bit more assertiveness to get the interview back on the rails. If it is tears you could say:

'I see you are very upset. Would you like 5 minutes to calm down and collect your thoughts? So-and-so can sit with you outside for 5 minutes if you like.'

Dealing with tears

(It's not a good idea to let somebody who is very upset go off on their own in the middle of an interview like this. They might disappear or they might create a lot of drama among other unprepared staff, either of which would be worrying and difficult to control.)

Dealing with anger

If it is anger, you could use:

'I see how angry you are, but we really cannot get anywhere until you calm down. I'd be glad if you would stop shouting [thumping the table, pacing around, whatever] and sit down so we can continue.'

'Play back' hooks

Avoid the hooks by 'playing them back'.

'I understand your fear that you won't get another job, but we must continue with what needs sorting out now.'

'I see how angry you are that you weren't told this before your holiday, but we must concentrate now on the matter in hand.'

'It's quite true that you have done some marvellous work in the last year. Sadly this doesn't alter the fact that today we have to sort your redundancy out.'

If the interviewee becomes very silent and shocked, you can again avoid getting hooked by showing that you observe this:

'I see you're shocked by this news at the moment. I'm going to move on now to the reasons we have to end your employment here, and to explain to you what you should do and what your rights are.'

If your interlocutor is dignified and assertive, this is a gift indeed, and means that you can get through the miserable business of terminating their employment and sorting out the necessary administration quickly and without drama or acrimony. The only risk for you is that, if they are absolutely admirable, you may start to get apologetic and passive. Watch out for it, and don't.

Don't apologise

If the worker is leaving then and there, it may be useful to have someone ready to escort them from the building. It is better to use someone else and not yourself as an escort, as it keeps the ending of your final meeting completely clear.

ESCORTING THE PERSON FROM THE BUILDING

The escort should however be properly briefed about their task. It must be done as an exercise of either assertive support if the person is very upset, or assertive containment if the person is very angry. Aggressive or indirectly aggressive behaviour should not be used. If the person leaving is predominantly angry, such behaviour will provoke further reaction. If the person leaving is predominantly distressed, it will be very damaging to them, because it will make them feel criminalised, and undercut any sensitivity with which the redundancy interview itself was carried out.

Don't be aggressive

After one or more members of staff have been made redundant, it is important to ensure that the shock waves that go through the rest of the staff are adequately dealt with. Call a staff meeting of the whole firm if you are a small to medium-sized firm, or of the department or section which had the redundancies if that is more appropriate. Tell them assertively what has happened and why, and, without aggression or threat, what you want from them in the future. Take questions and remain assertive, and then consider the matter closed. If at all possible send the workforce away with a sense that you have given them clear and accurate information, and with some positive target to aim at.

KEEPING REMAINING STAFF INFORMED

Keep good communication

GETTING SUPPORT FOR YOURSELF

Process your feelings

The final part of making people redundant assertively is taking care of yourself. If you went through the redundancy process with a colleague or colleagues you can give each other some support. If this feels impossible, it is certainly a time when the support of speaking partners, friends and significant others can be asked for and well used without any sense that you are making an unnecessary fuss.

An essential part of assertiveness is learning to recognise and acknowledge your own needs and seeking to fulfil them, and not to feel that if you were really tough you would not have any needs at all. It is perfectly reasonable to want to talk over, commiserate, review, discuss and generally process your feelings if you have had to make people redundant.

Leadership 7

Leaders may have Five Weaknesses:

The overly reckless can be destroyed.
The overly cautious can be captured.
The quickly angered can be ridiculed.
The very fastidious can be humiliated.
The deeply attached can be harassed.

Generally, the Five Weaknesses are a mistake in a leader.
   They are catastrophic in the execution of a strategy.
   If a Force is defeated and a leader destroyed, it is certainly
because of the Five Weaknesses.
   They must be carefully studied.

So wrote Sun Tzu, about 23 centuries ago, in his extraordinary
military treatise *The Art of Strategy*. His remarks reinforce the
conclusions we might draw today about assertiveness as a crucial
ingredient in effective leadership.
   Being overly reckless and being quickly angered are clearly
aggressive weaknesses, and being overly cautious and being very
fastidious are passive. Being 'deeply attached' is also a kind of
passivity – being deeply involved and caring about the outcome
in a destabilised, personalised way, in the end leads to the
possibility of a victim-like mentality. To a Taoist like Sun Tzu (or
any of the great martial arts instructors), being 'deeply attached'
is an error of strategy. For them, power and equilibrium lie in
observation without ego, and in good intuitive recognition of
'how things work'. As John Heider says in his interesting book

The Tao of Leadership (an interpretation of the ancient text the *Tao Te Ching*): 'remember ''Tao'' means ''how'' '.

So Sun Tzu picks out aggressive and passive behaviour as key weaknesses in leaders.

Effective leadership rests on assertive skills – on accurate, calm observation and on the model of power within.

POWER WITHIN

Transactional analysis is a way of describing and understanding behaviour which became popular in Europe and America in the 1970s and 1980s. It is particularly useful in helping to work out *why* an unsatisfactory transaction is unsatisfactory, and *why* a good transaction works. It suggests that we tend to behave in either the Parent, or the Adult, or the Child mode.

UNDERSTANDING THE TRANSACTION	
Characteristics	*Effects*
PARENT **Physical** Furrowed brow, pursed lips, the pointing index finger, head wagging, the 'horrified' look, foot tapping, hands on hips, arms folded across the chest. Wringing hands, tutting, interrupting others' speech.	Very often behaviour learned from own parents. Well-known parenting behaviour to evoke a child's response. Used to manipulate. Indirectly aggressive.
Verbal 'I'm going to put a stop to this once and for all.' 'You always do that.' 'I can't for the life of me ...' 'You never did!' 'How many times have I told you?' 'If I were you . . .' 'Poor thing', 'disgusting', 'naughty', 'ridiculous'. 'How dare you!' 'Should', 'ought'.	All aimed at influencing the behaviour of others, sometimes in an almost threatening way (bluff). 'Always' and 'never' are almost always Parent words which can reveal the limitations of an archaic system, resenting and rebuffing change. Judgmental, advice-giving from the 'if it were me . . .' stance.

UNDERSTANDING THE TRANSACTION – *contd.*	
Characteristics	*Effects*
CHILD **Physical** Tears, quivering lips, pouting, temper tantrums, rolling eyes, shrugging shoulders, teasing, downcast eyes, delight, laughter, hand raising for permission to speak, nail biting, squirming, giggling.	Child's earliest responses are non-verbal, so often a child's physical expressions are overt.
Verbal Baby talk 'I wish' 'I want' 'I dunno' 'I gonna' 'I don't care' 'bigger', 'biggest' 'better', 'best' 'later on', 'when I grow up'.	The need for attention, the need to impress. (The ever-questioning words – Why? When? Who? Where? and How? – often associated with the growing child are in fact an Adult response by a little person.)
ADULT **Physical** The active listener, nods, encouraging responses, not interrupting, eyes blinking every 3.5 seconds, sincere smiling, consistency of verbal and non-verbal messages.	To listen is an essential adult reaction. Empathy. Movement is essential to active listening. Reassuring touch.
Verbal The questioning words: Why? What? Who? Where? When? How? How much? In what way? 'True', 'false', 'probable', 'possible', 'unknown', 'objective', 'I think', 'I feel', 'I see', 'It is my opinion'.	The right to enquire and question, the learning processes to achieve maturity. Other words are non-judgemental offering words, subjective, opinions. Ownership of emotions ('I feel . . .').

They match closely with the concepts of aggressive, passive and assertive behaviours.

When you have to be a good leader it is useful to check with your own feelings that you are in the 'adult' role, and not the 'parent'. Check that you are:

- experiencing power within and not power over
- feeling responsibility *to* but not responsibility *for*
- in a balanced and alert physical state, not a tense and restless physical state.

The more you are in the 'adult', the more you will tend to bring out the 'adult' in your juniors. When you slip into the 'parent' they will tend to move into the 'child', or confront you with their own 'parent'.

BEING PROMOTED

The first challenge of leadership is being promoted into the leadership position in the first place. Because most organisations are pyramid-shaped, and because, especially in a recession, they are often *not* networking outwards as fast as staff are ready to take managerial positions, there is a bottleneck. At the bottleneck obviously there will be some people who do not make the breakthrough to the managerial tier. If you have made that breakthrough, you have to work out how to respond to the reaction of your peers, and how to re-negotiate your relationship with them.

'You can be as friendly, but you can't be as close.'

This is how one man summed up the change in his attitude to those who had been his peers when he was promoted to a senior managerial post. His plan was to be quite careful *not* to change his attitude to anyone in terms of friendliness and approachability. He did however decide that it was no longer appropriate for him to share his own vulnerability or the reasons behind some of his thinking with people who were now his subordinates. He felt that it was sensible and possible to remain in roughly the same personal style, but to be much more selective in sharing feelings and information with those people.

A number of hooks may come your way once you do move into the leadership position. They are motivated by two things:

- envy

- confusion over boundaries

Use basic assertiveness technique: **show you've heard, avoid the hook**, and **repeat the core phrase**.

For instance, an envious hook might be:

'Why don't you come out to the pub for lunch with us any more – aren't we good enough for you these days then?'

Said with sarcasm this is indirectly aggressive, and also signals that what is being said behind your back is probably, 'She's got very big for her boots all of a sudden', or 'Who does she think she is?'

Decide what you want to say and build a core phrase to express it. It might be:

'I'm sorry if it seems that way to you. Actually I was planning to come out for a drink with you all today. I don't have time to get there every day any longer.'

or it might be:

'I can see it might look that way, but I do need to use pretty well all my time catching up at the moment. I'll be joining you again sometime soon.'

Or you might want to get rid of the hook without giving any other promises or reasons:

'Not at all, I hope we're all good enough for each other! Now, let's get on with X.'

You do not have to accept criticisms which you disagree with, or apologise or give reasons for refusals unless it is professionally necessary or *you* want to (see p. 125).

A hook which comes from confusion about boundaries might be:

'I know you won't mind fixing this for me.'

– where your colleague assumes that now you're in a position of power you'll be 'looking after' old friends. You might want to say:

'I won't be fixing anything for anyone. In fact my aim is to get things done as well as possible through the normal channels.'

or, more gently,

'I can see why you think that might be possible, but we must get it straight that I won't. My intention is to do things fairly and by the book and that rules out favouritism and special pleading.'

Handling discipline and motivation

Disciplinary matters and motivational work are more difficult at first, until you are established in your new role and people have become accustomed to it.

'I can't believe I'm hearing this from you, Derek. Surely you're not trying to tell me this work isn't up to scratch. I mean, how long have we been friends?'

To which you might want to reply:

'We have been friends for several years, but the fact remains that this piece of work is not good enough, and you're going to have to re-do the last three pages.'

Or you might find a colleague saying,

'Oh, don't push me on this now for heaven's sake. It's Friday afternoon, can't we let it ride till Monday? You never used to be so bloody conscientious.'

You might want to reply:

'I know it's hard to keep your energy going on a Friday afternoon, but you must get this finished.'

– showing you heard the 'don't be so hard on me' hook, but choosing not to play back the 'you never used to be conscientious' one.

If you feel you must respond to the latter hook, whether because it's delivered with so much needle or for some other reason, you might choose something like,

'It's irrelevant these days how conscientious I was or wasn't in the past. I know it's hard to keep your energy going on a Friday afternoon . . .'

It will always be tricky, especially in the first few months, to handle the change in relationships and status which comes from being promoted into the managerial tier. You need to work out in your own mind what the new boundaries and attitudes are, and set the atmosphere, the language, the behaviour and the limits which you feel are right, in an assertive manner, and then if necessary defend them assertively too.

COMMUNICATION IN LEADERSHIP

Assertive communication in leadership is vital in the key areas:

- sharing the plan

- walking the job

- getting your boss to agree

'You can't expect people to care about something they know nothing about.' (Maya Winter, Marketing Adviser, Industrial Society)

SHARING THE PLAN

In your managerial role you may be able to exercise some influence over policy or 'the plan' – and will do so as effectively as you can.

Once the plan is formed and agreed, your task is different. For best motivation and best performance from your team you must share the plan clearly with them. The necessary steps are:

- reconcile yourself

- share as much information as you can

- be ready to explain and unpack

Reconcile yourself   You may have mixed feelings about some elements of the plan, but the team is not the place to share those feelings, unless you decide together to make a creative move to change it. More commonly, your role is to reconcile yourself with your feelings in whatever way works for you best. You could share doubts and frustrations with a speaking partner or friend, or simply use the discipline of putting them to one side.

What is *not* good practice is to let your team know that *you* feel equivocal about the plan but expect *them* to perform as though they were fully committed. Your team needs to feel your commitment to the plan and your intention to make it work. This is the most positive motivation you can provide. It does not have to consist of overt excitement. It could simply be clear-sighted and obvious determination and commitment.

Share information   Information is the currency of power in many organisations and you may feel a need to be aware of how much information you give and how much you withhold. You may feel as though you can never be spontaneously open. However, your equation should take into account how much junior managers and staff members hate having information withheld from them.

'It's like being drip-fed', said one junior manager in a firm of accountants, referring to his sense of being given minimum, rather than maximum information. This dissatisfaction was intense enough to be a key part of his decision to leave that firm.

As a general rule, share as much information as you can when leading a team: the team members' sense of involvement and of being trusted and respected will increase their motivation, while any sense of being not trusted, not respected and not informed would do the reverse.

Be ready to explain   You are the first-line resource for your team. Be ready to explain or unpack the detail of implementation when you share the plan, and to do so in an assertive or adult-to-adult style. Teaching and learning in this positive management mood become part of a mutually respectful working partnership.

WALKING THE JOB

'Walking the job' is a good practice to consider mapping into your management strategy. The advantage is that your team have a sense of you spending some time alongside them in the genuine context of their job. If you manage large numbers of people it ensures that they know who you are and you know who they are. It reduces the risk of remoteness between a large workforce and a senior manager.

You become a real person with whom communication is possible. You also become a real identity on behalf of whom one might choose to make an extra effort, or meet a deadline, or be pleased to report an extra sale or contract.

The managing director of a chain of shoe shops chose to devote one day per week visiting branches. He kept a file on personnel in each branch with photographs and details important *to that person* so that he was able to arrive, recognise and know the names of staff, and ask questions about their interests and concerns, both about commercial matters and in the area of their children, or their sporting interests, or whatever was important to them. This produced a strong bonding with his staff, which was reflected in low staff turnover and good growth of staff up through the organisation: a strong overall loyalty.

Lord Seiff records in his autobiography his practice of ringing a Marks and Spencer branch manager towards the end of a

Saturday afternoon's trading to find out what sort of day it had
been in his or her branch, how the takings had been, which lines
were performing and so forth. It was a tremendous shot in the
arm for staff at the most exhausting moment of the retail week
to have direct contact with the chief and direct interest in their
specific branch and its achievements and concerns, and was an
interesting strand in Marks and Spencer's impressive package of
staff care.

These are two examples of walking the job where the
managers wished to raise their profile and improve performance
and productivity by having a direct and rather electric contact
with their staff. Walking the job can also be done incognito, in
which case it can be used as a diagnostic tool. You can find out
things as a member of the workforce that you would never hear
when perceived as a person in a suit who never gets her or his
hands dirty.

One managing director is an 'assistant lorry driver' one day a
month at different branches and locations. On these days he
sees and hears the 'real' company, which it is unlikely he would
otherwise have access to.

A film director described how, on occasion, he did his own
motorcycle courier work. He was able to pick up all sorts of
insights about the industry, the competition, the rumours and
the buzz, with a penetration that would not happen when he was
in his office.

Information and impressions gathered on undercover 'walking
the job' enrich your understanding of what is going on in your
organisation. The deeper your understanding is, the more clearly
you can target areas which need your assertive action or
reaction.

To lead your team well, you need to be able to get your issues as
a team heard and handled by your boss. The presentation of the
problem and your suggested solution should come as steadily
and levelly as any core phrase, with an emphasis on the adult–
adult, win–win aspect and avoidance of passive (please rescue
me) or aggressive (bloody well listen) language.

The real learning point here is to make your boss feel that you
are presenting him or her not primarily with a problem, but with
a solution. To help ensure a problem gets fair consideration, it
should be systematically thought through and well presented –
accurately, briefly and clearly (see the guidelines on p. 110).

GETTING YOUR BOSS TO AGREE

DEALING WITH TEAM PROBLEMS

1 State the problem
Make sure it really is the problem you are stating and not a symptom (e.g. 'the post is often late arriving on your desk' could be a symptom of poor organisation of the post room or messenger services).

2 Identify the adverse effects and disadvantages
Try to quantify the effects, where possible, in terms of time lost, unnecessary cost, material wasted, low output, evidence of effect on staff morale, etc.

3 List possible solutions (if more than one)
Consider listing pros and cons in two columns so as to make them easily comparable. If it is appropriate, attach supporting evidence, in visual form if possible, e.g. graphs, diagrams, tables, flow charts.

4 Make your recommendation
State which you have decided is the best solution, with the benefits in cost, time, morale, etc., and ask for the boss's agreement.

There are two main advantages of a systematic approach to putting up recommendations:

(a) **to the boss** . . .
who does not have to do any investigation: the options are there, ready for evaluation; the decision is simplified and is usually limited to agreeing or disagreeing.

(b) **to the individual** . . .
who has to sit down, analyse the problem and think through how best to deal with it.

The spin-off is that bosses value those individuals who can demonstrate the ability to work out problems for themselves more highly than those who just present problems for someone else to handle.

SELF-MANAGEMENT

'It's the easiest thing in the world to be busy. What's difficult is to be effective.'

Ask yourself – are you mostly busy, or are you mostly effective? If you work in a 'panic culture' where people validate themselves by rushing, blustering, working late and early, and verbalising a great deal about pressure, it may be extra difficult to arrive at a good answer to this question.

Good self-management is a matter of being assertive with *yourself* and ensuring that you are effective rather than busy. This can be achieved in many ways, but we will focus here on three concepts which are useful. They are:

- urgent or important?

- who's holding the problems?

- 'mens sana in corpore sano' (a sound mind in a sound body)

Becoming less busy and more effective is often a matter of learning to prioritise. A useful matrix to use to measure the weighting you should give certain tasks is to ask yourself whether you think they are urgent or important:

URGENT OR IMPORTANT?

- **Urgent** matters require immediate attention, have a quick disaster potential if nothing is done, and have short-term implications anywhere on a scale from trivial to serious.

- **Important** matters require attention in the near future, will not come to crisis quickly if nothing is done, but have serious long-term implications in terms of policy, or structure, or development, or career progress.

It is immediately clear that, as a manager, one all too often spends 99 per cent of the time on urgent fire-fighting and 1 per cent on important business. Positive leadership of your team involves becoming alert to this danger, and ensuring that you spend sufficient time on the *important* issues to keep the team alive, moving, protected and developing, and decrease the time you spend on *urgent* issues by delegating as many of them as possible down the line.

Time management skills (available to managers now through numerous books and courses), put into practice with good assertive communication, will help you to maintain this distinction between the urgent and the important. In doing so you are organising your own activities in a way which is assertive on behalf of your team.

WHO'S HOLDING THE PROBLEMS?

As a manager, you are the linking agent between directors and workers. Either group can at any time present you with problems to deal with: the problems of the organisation. If you feel you are holding enormous numbers of problems from both sides, you can start to feel paralysed, overstressed and ineffective. Develop your assertive self-management by:

(a)   holding only those problems you really feel you should hold, and

(b)   when you want to and it is appropriate, leaving the problems behind.

Holding problems   There are all sorts of problems you must hold, because it is your job. You must sort out personality clashes in your team, you must respond to and organise for their training needs, and so forth. However, there are times when you do not have to take the problem on. It may not be within your role to disentangle another person's mistake, or support their chaotic project, or go beyond a certain point in involvement with their personal problems.

Be assertive about your boundaries

If you assert your boundaries, you avoid compromising your leadership by becoming overstressed. When someone comes into your room with a problem, visualise it as a small, troublesome, agile animal, like a monkey, sitting on their shoulder. There is the problem, metaphorically animated. What they want is for it to jump off their shoulder, scamper across your desk, and climb onto your shoulder. They then walk away lighter and freer, and you remain in your room, heaving a sigh. On a bad Monday morning you might have half-a-dozen monkeys sitting chattering on your shoulders by 9 o'clock!

If you really feel that a 'monkey' that somebody brings you is not part of your job to take care of, make sure it stays on their shoulder, and they walk away clearly understanding that they must take care of it themselves. Without needing to share the monkey metaphor, use assertive core phrases to explain what you are doing.

Leaving problems behind   It is essential to be able to leave problems to one side in order to deal with other parts of the job, and it is essential to be able to leave problems to one side in order to live fully the other parts of one's life.

Put problems 'to bed'

Visualise the problems once again as monkeys. Do everything you need to do to make them comfortable: feed them, water them and give them a comfortable box of straw to sleep in. Then they will not chatter and distract you. That is to say, do everything you feel is appropriate about a problem for the time being, and then believe that you can safely leave the problem alone while you get on with something else.

When you go home, make active, assertive choices about which monkeys to take home with you. Leave as many as you can at the office, and take any home only those you want to work on. Work either actively or subconsciously on those you do take home. Decide to spend time at a desk, or decide to let a problem float freely around in your mind; and then decide when you are going to leave it altogether. If you are visualising a problem as a monkey, put it to sleep in its straw box. If you see it as something else, create in your own mind an image to contain it. A housing benefits manager whose working life is overrun with extremely fraught problems says:

> 'I was sleeping progressively worse and worse, because problems would intrude on me as I slept and wake me. I trained myself, on the way to bed, to imagine a large box at the bottom of the stairs. I imagined all the problems written on bits of paper and dropped into the box, and then, the lid, which I imagine as very heavy, shutting down on them. They can't get out. I walk away from the box quite clear that I won't open it again till morning.'

Use any image that helps you to put your problems away when you want to sleep or do anything else in your private life which matters to you.

Assertive choice and containment of problems make you a more effective leader.

Suppose somebody gave you a car – free. They said, this is for you, and you can have it, for nothing. Imagine your delight. You ask if there's a catch, or a trick, or a snag. They say, no, not at all, this is for you and you can have it: but there is just one thing to remember – you can never, ever have another one.

Notice how your immediate reaction is, well, I must be very careful to look after this one then. This story demonstrates exactly the position you are in with regard to your body: it is yours for free, but you can never have another one, so you must take care of the one you have got. Without it, you cannot be a manager of any kind, never mind an assertive one.

Maintaining health, stamina and well-being (see *Are You Managing Your Health?* by H. Beric Wright) has to be a basic brick in your managerial strategy, not just an optional, peripheral, I'll

MENS SANA

Take care of your body

do something about it when it reaches crisis point, extra. You cannot lead your team if you are in hospital with a perforated ulcer or at home with unmanageable panic attacks. Body, mind and spirit have to be at least in workable equilibrium to empower you in your professional capacity.

Many courses and books elucidate good thinking and practice in the area of stress management. It might be an important part of your management development to assign some time to these subjects.

ACTION-CENTRED LEADERSHIP

Any group will expect its leader to have certain qualities but they will vary with individual perceptions. There is no standard mix of qualities, let alone definitions for the perfect leader. Leadership effectiveness can come from assertive communication within an action-centred structure.

LEADERSHIP ACTIONS

The leader is employed to get a job done through the efforts of individual human beings, working as a team. The leader therefore has three interrelated areas in which to work, irrespective of the level of management:

- develop individuals

- build the team

- achieve the task

John Adair's action-centred model demonstrates that, by developing and motivating individuals to get things done through teamwork, we become effective leaders. A breakdown or neglect of one area will affect the others, preventing the job being done as effectively as it could be. The checklists on pp.

115–16 highlight the important questions to ask yourself about task, team and individuals in order to attend fully to all three.

The model action plan on p. 117 will help you with any task over which you want to exercise leadership that is both action centred and assertive.

CHECKLISTS FOR TASK, TEAM AND INDIVIDUALS

TASK

PURPOSE:	Am I clear what the task is?
RESPONSIBILITIES:	Am I clear as to what mine are?
OBJECTIVES:	Have I agreed these with my boss for the team?
PLAN:	Have I worked one out to reach objectives?
WORKING CONDITIONS:	Are these right for the job?
RESOURCES:	Are these adequate (authority, money, materials)?
TARGETS:	Has each member clearly defined and agreed them?
THE LEADER:	Do people know who they report to?
AUTHORITY:	Are all lines of authority clear (accountability chart)?
TRAINING:	Are there any gaps in the team's abilities?
PRIORITIES:	Have I planned the time?
PROGRESS:	Do I check this regularly and evaluate?
DEPUTY:	In case of absence who covers?
EXAMPLE:	Do I set high standards by my own behaviour?
WALK THE JOB:	Do I monitor at the place of work?

TEAM

OBJECTIVES:	Does the team understand them?
STANDARDS:	Do they know what is expected?
QUALITY:	Have the appropriate standards been agreed?
SAFETY:	Do they know consequences of infringement?
SIZE OF TEAM:	Is the number correct (4–15)?

continued

TEAM – *contd.*

TEAM MEMBERS:	Are the right people working together?
TEAM SPIRIT:	Is the job structured to encourage this?
DISCIPLINE:	Are the rules seen to be reasonable and applied fairly?
GRIEVANCES:	Are these dealt with promptly?
CONSULTATION:	Is this genuine? Do I encourage any ideas and suggestions?
BRIEFING:	Is this regular?
TRADE UNIONS:	Does the team know the organisation's attitudes?
BACK-UP:	Are there regular team meetings?

INDIVIDUALS

TARGETS:	Have they been set and quantified?
INDUCTION:	Do they really know the organisation?
ACHIEVEMENT:	Do they know their work contribution?
RESPONSIBILITIES:	Have they got a job description?
AUTHORITY:	Do they have sufficient for their responsibilities?
TRAINING:	Has adequate provision been made?
RECOGNITION:	Do I emphasise people's successes?
GROWTH:	Do they see the chance of development?
PERFORMANCE:	Is this regularly reviewed?
REWARD:	Are work capacity and pay in balance?
THE TASK:	Are they in the right job?
THE PERSON:	Do I know the person well?
TIME/ATTENTION:	Do I spend enough time listening?
GRIEVANCES:	Are these dealt with promptly?
SECURITY:	Do they know about pensions, redundancy, etc.?
WALK THE JOB:	Do I support and catch people doing things right?

ACTION PLANNING FOR LEADERSHIP			
Key Actions	*Task*	*Team*	*Individual*
Define objectives	Identify tasks & constraints	Hold team meetings Share commitment	Clarify objectives Gain acceptance
Plan — Gather information	Consider options Check resources	Consult Encourage ideas Develop suggestions Assess skills	
Plan — Decide	Priorities Time scales Standards	Structure	Allocate jobs Delegate Set targets
Brief	Clarify objectives Describe plan	Explain decisions Listen Answer questions Enthuse Check understanding	
Monitor Support	Assess progress Maintain standards	Coordinate Reconcile conflict	Advise Assist/reassure Counsel Discipline
		Recognise effort	
Evaluate	Summarise progress Review objectives Re-plan if necessary	Recognise & gain from success Learn from mistakes	
		Guide & train Give praise	

In order to evaluate the condition of your team, regularly use the checklist on these two pages.

CHARACTERISTICS OF EFFECTIVE AND INEFFECTIVE TEAMS	
Effective teams	*Ineffective teams*
1. The atmosphere tends to be informal, comfortable. People are involved and interested.	1. The atmosphere reflects either indifference or boredom (people whispering to each other, etc.)
2. There is a lot of discussion in which everyone takes part. Everyone keeps to the point.	2. Only a few people talk. Little effort is made to keep to the point of the discussion.
3. Everybody understands the task they have to do.	3. It is difficult to understand what the group task is.
4. The group members listen to each other. Every idea is given a hearing.	4. People do not really listen to each other. Some ideas are not put forward to the group.
5. There is disagreement. The group is comfortable with this, and they work together towards sorting it out. Nobody feels unhappy with decisions made.	5. Disagreements are not dealt with effectively. They are put to the vote without being discussed. Some people are unhappy with decisions.
6. People feel free to criticise and say honestly what they think.	6. People are not open about what they are thinking. They grumble about decisions afterwards.
7. Everybody knows how everybody else feels about what is being discussed.	7. One or two people are dominant. What they say goes!
8. When action needs to be taken, everyone is clear about what has to be done, and they help each other.	8. Nobody takes any interest in what has to be done, and they do not offer to help others.

continued

continued

Effective teams	Ineffective teams
9. Different people take over the role of leader from time to time.	9. Only one or two people make the decisions and act as group leaders.
10. The group is conscious of how well it is working and of what is interfering with its progress. It can look after itself.	10. The group does not talk about how it is working or about the problems it is facing. It needs someone to look after it.

MOTIVATION

What motivates staff to work well? Leaders can make assumptions about people at work. In the extreme these can be described as X and Y below. Consider which assumptions you tend to make.

ASSUMPTIONS ABOUT PEOPLE AT WORK	
Extreme 'X'	*Extreme* 'Y'
People dislike work and will avoid it if they can.	People will direct themselves towards accepted targets.
People must be forced to produce the right effort.	The targets people set for themselves are more effective and often more demanding than those imposed on them.
People are motivated mainly by money.	Work is a necessary part of people's personal development.
People would rather be directed than accept authority.	People have considerable creativity and ingenuity, which are grossly underused.
People will work harder when they fear their job is under threat.	Under the right conditions people will seek, and accept, authority.
People have little creativity except for getting round management rules.	People want to be interested in their work and, under the right conditions, want to enjoy it.

If X is to be our assumption, and we treat people accordingly, we find out nothing about them because our beliefs become a self-fulfilling prophecy; i.e. people will need close supervision, firm discipline, incentive schemes and continued pressing for results.

If, however, we believe that Y is correct, and treat people accordingly, we will find out what they are really like. We will find that people are different and will respond to the leadership actions in building on individual strengths and minimising weaknesses.

The key is not to make assumptions but to give opportunities for achievement, responsibility and creativity for each individual team member to develop to their full potential. Our coaching, supporting and recognition will then result in getting the best from people.

Practical steps in motivation   Once a certain standard of living is achieved, more than money is needed to increase an individual's contribution. A leader must be aware of how to get people to work willingly and well in order to increase the individual's satisfaction in the job and the organisation's efficiency.

LEADERSHIP METHODOLOGY

Make people feel valued by:

- regularly monitoring and appreciating each subordinate's work

- sharing an interest in whatever they hold important

- creating a good working environment by being approachable

- ensuring everyone understands the importance of their contribution to the team's objectives

- ensuring everyone understands the function of the organisation, and why industry matters

Provide a challenge and scope for development by:

- setting targets, after consultation, and reviewing them at regular intervals

---

continued

continued

- providing relevant training – where appropriate by using people to train others in the specialist skills they may have

- arranging any necessary internal and external contacts

- restructuring or grouping tasks to use people's skills to the fullest

- rotating jobs to broaden experience

- providing scope for individuals to take greater responsibility

- training thoroughly at least one deputy

- encouraging ideas and suggestions and listening; by delegating and allowing staff to take decisions and to implement them

Recognise achievements by:

- praising and communicating individual successes

- reporting regularly to the team on their progress

- holding regular meetings with each individual to monitor and counsel progress

Communicate by:

- explaining the organisation's results and achievements

- setting and communicating the team's objectives and regularly appraising them of its progress

- ensuring the team know how the organisation is doing

- communicating any changes taking place in the organisation

- explaining decisions to assist people to accept them

This simple and clear analysis of leadership methodology shows the action-centred structure through which an assertive style of communication can operate at its best.

Let us leave the last word on leadership to Jon Heider. His view is that accurate and flexible leadership loses its stresses

and strains and becomes a process of facilitation. You may agree
or disagree, but either way his hypothesis will give you food for
thought:

> The greatest martial arts are the softest. They allow an
> attacker the opportunity to fall down. The greatest generals
> do not rush into every battle. They offer the enemy many
> opportunities to make self-defeating errors.
>
> The greatest administrators do not achieve production
> through constraints and limitations. They provide
> opportunities.
>
> Good leadership consists of motivating people to their
> highest levels by offering them opportunities, not obligations.
>
> This is how things happen naturally. Life is an opportunity
> and not an obligation.
>
> (*The Tao of Leadership*, section 68)

Coping with Criticism, Enjoying Praise   8

YOU will regularly be on the receiving end of evaluative
comment from bosses, peers, subordinates and clients. You
also have to make evaluative comments for your staff, to help
them to work out how they are doing and where they stand.

Giving criticism in a way which helps to alter things for the
better, and receiving criticism in a similarly positive way, involves
an assertive element. The same is true of the pleasanter
business of hearing positive feedback in a way which empowers
you, and giving positive feedback so that it has an optimum
effect on raising morale and performance.

Let us look first at the assertive management of negative or
difficult comment.

RECEIVING CRITICISM WELL

One of the most empowering things assertiveness can do for us
is to enable us to hear criticism without feeling destroyed.

To understand why this is, we need to understand why
criticism sometimes *does* feel devastating. When we were young,
we were often criticised by parents or guardians, teachers or
other powerful adults in our lives. That criticism would often take
the form:

'You are stupid.'

'You are lazy.'
'You are spiteful.'

and so on.

The child or young person takes this information as true data, and believes that he or she *is* stupid, or lazy, or spiteful. Their self-esteem plummets, and there is not much constructive they can do about the criticism, since the implication is that the fault is intrinsic in them. The learned feeling is that criticism hurts and leaves you feeling helpless.

It is a different matter if the criticiser has the sense or skill to say,

'That was a stupid thing to do.'
'That is a lazy way to behave.'
'That was a spiteful thing to do.'

Learn to hear criticism as behaviour specific

These statements are behaviour-specific; they suggest not that there is a personality fault, but that there is a piece of behaviour which is misguided or mistaken. The criticisms may not be a lot of fun to hear, but the person hearing them does not feel written off. They can see what they need to change to alter the sorts of comments that they get. The learned feeling is that criticism may not be comfortable, but you can choose to do something about it.

Any sense of collapse or destruction you feel when receiving criticism probably dates back to feelings of helplessness and hopelessness experienced when being criticised as a little child. You can begin to dismantle such reactions by remembering to separate the criticised behaviour out as a distinct thing in itself. This involves being able to hear,

'You have made a mess of this task.'

without thinking it means either,

'You always make a mess of every task.'

or

'You are completely incompetent.'

DO YOU AGREE?

Once you have worked out how to hear a behaviour–specific criticism without collapsing, you can check whether you agree with it or not.

If you agree, make an assertive statement of it,

'Yes, I think that's true. I did make a mess of that task.'

Repeat the words of the criticism more or less exactly in your assertive agreement – it makes it much more powerful.

Don't start explaining, or justifying, or apologising (you can do those things later if you want to). Keep it short and clear. Remember from the Bill of Rights (p. 45) that everyone has the right to make mistakes. Don't roll in the dirt. Simply agree.

This puts you in a strong and self-respecting position to start negotiating about how to repair or improve matters.

If you disagree, then make an assertive statement to that effect, again repeating the words of the criticism more or less exactly to make your statement focused and powerful.

> 'No, I don't agree with that. I haven't made a mess of that task.'

Don't explain, or justify, or argue, at this point. You can do those things later if you want to. Keep it short and clear, thus clearing the ground for an adult–adult discussion of the problem situation.

If you don't know whether you agree or disagree, say so, and ask for time for reflection if it is practical to do so.

> 'I'm surprised to hear you say that. I'd like to think it over before I respond.'

> 'I'm amazed; that's not how I saw it at all. Can you leave it with me for a bit while I take in what you've said.'

Coping with criticism can be developed further by:

- learning how to 'fog'
- identifying your 'crumple buttons'
- adding an assertive 'rider'

General criticism can be particularly difficult to deal with. It is hard to identify exactly what is wrong and it is therefore difficult to have a constructive discussion about it. This is particularly pertinent with regard to formal appraisal systems, and several clear distinctions can be made between (less useful) *criticism* and (more useful) *feedback* (see pp. 132–3). If you are faced with a criticism which is highly general, such as:

> 'Your attitude is all wrong.'

> 'You aren't dynamic enough.'

> 'Your communication is so poor.'

LEARNING HOW TO 'FOG'

use the 'fogging' technique to find out what is at the bottom of it.

Don't argue

Don't argue with the criticism – 'fog' over it with a 'maybe' or a 'perhaps' – and a question which tracks the specific.

Track the specific criticism

'Maybe my attitude does need revising. Can you say exactly what it is that concerns you about it?'

'Perhaps I'm not communicating well at the moment. It would be helpful if you could give me an example of what you mean.'

This should enable the criticiser to be specific:

'I'm worried about the way you dress when you meet new clients. It doesn't reflect the image I want this Company to have. That's what I mean by your attitude: that's what concerns me about it.'

'When I say you're not dynamic I'm thinking about things like how slow you've been to respond to client Y. It really isn't good enough to take 10 days to get a quote out; they have probably gone to someone else by now.'

'Well I was furious to find that the first your department knew about so-and-so being replaced was to see her job being advertised in the paper. And how do you think she felt? You *must* organise yourself better than that.'

Now you know exactly what the specific issues are upon which you are being challenged.

It might take several goes, but as with re-thinking the core phrase when necessary, just keep going until you get there.

'I don't like your style, it's not right at all.'

'Maybe there is a problem with my style; can you say what it is that bothers you about it?'

'Well, it's your style with suppliers I'm thinking of really.'

'Can you think of an example of what you mean? Or just give me a bit more detail?'

'Well, what you do is you're too easily fobbed off. I hear you on the phone and you are so understanding and soft with them, when we really need those supplies. It compromises our output not to have them on time and it seems to me you swallow any old excuse. I think you have got to be much more abrasive and make it clear they are not to mess you about.'

Now the thing is focused, you can begin to respond to it. It is important not to argue with or challenge the criticism at all until you have refined it down to a specific; it is a waste of time and energy discussing something that is nebulous, and may both sour the atmosphere and defuse your energy. Save your assertive reaction for the true central issue.

Respond to the specific criticism

A 'crumple-button' is an area around which you cannot *bear* to be criticised – you instantly *crumple*. The origin of this phenomenon probably also goes back well into the past.

IDENTIFYING YOUR 'CRUMPLE-BUTTONS'

A criticism from a particularly withering teacher, or a taunting sibling or a scornful parent can sensitise certain areas for you for life! Our assertive option is to recognise these highly sensitised areas, and to receive criticism in those areas particularly carefully, being tender with ourselves.

Everybody has 'crumple-buttons'. It is useful to work out what yours are.

You may be extremely civilised and adult dealing with criticism of your written style or your personal presentation, but feel that if anyone so much as hints that you are putting on weight you will either go berserk or break down and sob. Perhaps you have taken in and learned from difficult critical feedback about your interpersonal skills, but feel that if someone criticises your standard of accuracy you will take an axe to their head. That is how you identify a crumple button – it is where your level of reaction to criticism is way out of proportion to the criticism itself.

Five short steps help to deal with 'crumple-button' criticisms:

1 notice the imminent criticism
2 breathe
3 contact your strength
4 respond assertively
5 congratulate yourself

1 Notice criticism coming In fact we are so highly sensitised to our 'crumple button' areas that we *do* sense the approach of an imminent criticism. Muscle-tensing, stomach-churning, all the familiar stress responses, flag up to you that someone is about to enter your 'crumple-button' zone.

2 Do not stop breathing It is a normal fear reaction to take a gulp of breath and hold onto it. You can maintain your composure far better if you manage to keep a steady flow of breath, and you can think more clearly too (your brain needs oxygen to work well). Make sure you breathe out: all animals will automatically breathe in, so, as long as you remember to exhale, your rhythm of breath will continue.

3 Contact your strength   Remind yourself of something which you know clearly you are good at. Really acknowledge it.

4 Make your assertive response   However mechanical it feels, it will serve you well in preserving your dignity and keeping the discussion on the rails.

5 Congratulate yourself   At the end of the encounter, remember to say 'well done' to yourself for getting through what was, for you, a difficult time, however trivial it may have looked to anybody else.

ADDING AN ASSERTIVE RIDER

If you agree with a criticism, you may want to add a positive rider to show that you are already alert to the problem and active about it.

> 'Yes, I agree that I did rush the material at that meeting. I have noticed that I tend to do that, and I am working on it.'

> 'Yes, I think I should have prepared the background better before seeing the client. I've certainly taken that in and I'll make sure my preparation is complete in the future.'

If you disagree with a criticism, you may want to add a positive rider with some specific counter-examples. Present them with a light touch as a matter of fact and without getting into an argument.

> 'No, I don't agree with you on that, I think I *do* take development initiatives myself. For example, this month I did a, b, and c, on the development side.'

Stop there, do not fall into the temptation of saying 'that proves it' or 'so how dare you'. Do not develop the point at length. Keep it brief and clear.

An assertive rider can also be useful when someone makes a comment that you agree with, but which they see as a criticism and you do not necessarily interpret in that light. Point out that you see it as something positive.

> 'Yes I agree that I often do get confidences out of people. I'm inclined to see that as an asset rather than a defect though.'

When you have worked on receiving criticism well, it is easier to *make* criticism constructively.

Making criticism so that it is useful, constructive and can be heard is covered in the section on appraisals.

COPING WITH PRAISE WELL

It may seem strange to need to spend time considering this point, but on reflection you will probably notice that you often 'waste' praise by rushing on and not allowing yourself to notice it, let alone bask in it and be positively encouraged by it.

The inhibiting factors are:

- cultural embarrassment

- doubting the source

- fearing a backlash

CULTURAL EMBARRASSMENT

Particularly in the UK, an ironic detachment is expected of professionals. Possibly this has class connections dating back to the aristocratic contempt for 'trade' and the cult of the amateur. To care too much, to appear to be too involved, too personally committed, is still tinged with some kind of cultural stigma. This can make accepting positive feedback awkward. However, allowing positive feedback to register properly can have such a beneficial effect on morale and energy that it is well worth trying to unpick that piece of cultural conditioning simply by beginning to be aware of it.

DOUBTING THE SOURCE

Why is this person giving me praise and support now? What do they want? What are they trying to flatter me into or distract me from? Is this the nice 'softener' that precedes a really nasty blow?

It is true that somebody may give positive feedback insincerely and from ulterior motives. However, they may be perfectly genuine.

FEARING A BACKLASH

There is an ancient Greek epigram,

'Against whom is this eulogy directed?'

Being singled out for praise was thought to be extremely dangerous, as it made one conspicuous and therefore vulnerable to jealous gods and humans alike.

A really spectacular piece of positive feedback may leave you feeling vulnerable to a backlash from envious peers. However, if you accept it assertively this is far less likely to happen.

So, if some positive feedback does come your way:

1   check the source
2   hear the praise
3   accept it without rushing
4   remember it – don't forget it or rubbish it later

1 Checking the source   One does have to make a balanced judgement about whether the praise is genuine or is part of a devious crusade of some sort. However, don't let paranoia spoil genuine positive feedback for you.

2 and 3 Hear the praise and accept it without rushing it
Listen to what the person is saying. Do not let your embarrassment cause you to hurry them on to another subject, or brush off what they are trying to tell you ('no, no, it was nothing'). Let the positive feedback hang in the air for a moment so that you really hear it.

If you feel the source is OK – that you respect the person and there is **no** ulterior motive for what they are saying – then accept it. Believe it.

4 Remember it and do not rubbish it afterwards   Add it to the store of information which helps you to remain confident about yourself. Resist the urge to dismantle it afterwards with –

'I don't suppose they meant it.'

or

'They would have said the same to anyone.'

When you have become practised at receiving positive feedback well, it becomes easier to *give* positive feedback in the way in which it can be most effective in changing and motivating the workforce.

APPRAISAL SYSTEMS

Most organisations now incorporate a formal appraisal system in their plan. The inclusion of such schemes reflects an increasing awareness of quality control, which has been developing through the 1980s and is now focused by the requirements of BS 5750.

It also reflects growing consciousness of a need to manage the human resource level well in any business. More appraisal systems now have the following objectives:

To enable the individual to:

- know how well he/she has performed in the past

- understand what he/she has to do to progress

- make plans for development

To enable the organisation to:

- identify individual capabilities

- make maximum use of individuals' capabilities

- communicate its views to an individual

To work well to improve staff performance and motivation, an appraisal system has to be congruent with the organisational culture in which it is embedded. Current thinking is that it is useful to keep *ideographic* appraisal – that is, retrospective performance review and prospective objective setting – separate from *nomothetic* appraisal, which is salary review. If the two happen together, the staff member does not hear the ideographic information clearly because he or she finds it hard not to worry about the nomothetic information.

Before concentrating on giving feedback in an appraisal interview we need to be aware of **two provisos**: the timing of formative feedback, and the amount of 'air time' the interviewer has.

Timing   Behaviourists would say that formative feedback, i.e. feedback which actually changes the way people behave next time, should be time-targeted:

- *negative* or critical feedback should be given just prior to the next occurrence of the criticised activity, so that the person has maximum information and opportunity to do it in a different way.

- *positive* feedback or praise should be given immediately after the praised activity so that the staff member makes maximum linkage between the way they performed and the pleasant feeling of being praised.

So, although much exchange of feedback takes place within appraisal systems, it is useful to remember to reinforce it well on a day-to-day basis by using time-targeted reminders.

Who gets the 'air time'?   Many managers giving staff appraisal interviews feel that they ought to have about 80 per cent of the speaking time, but this behaviour does not pass feedback on in the most effective way. If the staff member has time to interact with responses and discuss the feedback, they 'hear' it, register it and understand it far more clearly, so it has a better chance of being formative. Do not be afraid of pauses and silences while the interviewee digests what is being said. One survey suggests that an effective interviewer should try not to take more than 25 per cent of the speaking time.
than 25 per cent of the speaking time.

When you have worked on receiving criticism well, it is easier to *make* criticism constructively.

In the assertive model of giving critical feedback, as always, body language should be in the relaxed/alert range, rather than the tense/fight or flight spectrum, and an assertive rather than an aggressive or passive tone and choice of words is more effective.

Look at the table below for a clear distinction between useful critical feedback and critical feedback that is difficult to use.

Useful critical feedback must be information that a subordinate can:

- accept

- understand

- do something about

Useful critical feedback is:	Critical feedback that is difficult to use is:
specific	general
descriptive	evaluative
remedy-seeking	blame-seeking
based in the present and future	based in the past
clear	fuzzy
tough on the issues	tough on the person
well timed	timed according to giver's needs
checked for understanding	'dumped'

Be ready to field panic reactions and/or aggression from the receiver of critical feedback, by using core phrases which re-focus them on the specific issues.

In particular, be ready to agree a manageable and specific number of future objectives which give the staff member an opportunity to change the criticised behaviour. They then form a hopeful rather than a hopeless mind-set about the issue in hand.

Positive feedback also needs to be given in an assertive way. Body language, again, needs to be in the relaxed/alert range and not the tense/fight or flight zone. The voice quality should be even and steady and praise must be given without envy or being patronising. In a study of praise and blame in appraisal interviews, it was found that praise was usually vague and general, and had little effect.

GIVING POSITIVE FEEDBACK ASSERTIVELY

Useful positive feedback is:

- **specific** – pick particular tasks, achievements, or qualities to praise

- **focused** – choose the words you use as precisely and carefully as you can: this tells your staff member that you thought carefully and perceived exactly what it was about their work that you want to pick out for positive feedback.

Immediate and rewarding feedback is a strong stimulus for improvement. If you are fairly senior in your field you may have forgotten what a crucial part of sustaining the learning process it is – but check it out against your need for praise and encouragement in any new sport, skill or activity you are trying to learn (note that the literal derivation of encouragement is 'giving heart to'). Senior staff members may not need quite so much praise and encouragement over learning new skills, but they emphatically do need praise and encouragement for their effort and commitment.

Most employees, and indeed most bosses, feel that they do not get anything like enough meaningful positive feedback. Everyone would benefit greatly from more thoughtful and clear interactions of this kind.

9 *Assertiveness in Equal Opportunities and Cross-Cultural Work*

*W*ᴇ have already seen the importance of using assertiveness to manage change. It has great value in breaking new ground, renegotiating old contacts and relationships, and handling anxiety.

Two issues which are generating a great deal of change in most workplaces are the increasing implementation of proper equal opportunities policies, and the growth of European and indeed transworld networking and trade. Both issues necessitate disciplined review of current attitudes and assumptions. These attitudes may be deeply embedded both in the organisational culture and in personal value systems, and may consequently be difficult and even painful to examine. Assertiveness can be used to facilitate the reviews of both a personal and an organisational level, and to work on the changes as well.

You may need to defend or confront or actively manage behaviour around these issues. Assertiveness is a positive asset if you need to do this.

Let us consider the various angles which might arise, starting with the applications of assertiveness to equal opportunities issues.

EQUAL OPPORTUNITIES ISSUES

When an organisation begins to face up to its responsibilities with respect to equal opportunity legislation it will probably have a difficult time.

The equal opportunity laws attempt to create a framework within which employment, training and development are equally available to everyone, whatever their sex, marital status, race and ability status. Some organisations in addition include in their internal equal opportunities policy specification for equal opportunities with regard to sexuality.

The formal systems and the informal culture of an organisation often have to change quite considerably to progress towards a point where there really is good equal opportunities practice. To make that progress people will have to think over questions about race, about sex and sexuality, about how families work. They will have to analyse their use of ordinary language, slang and body language, they will have to put their own social skills under the microscope, and they will have to think through the assumptions they make about colleagues and the public based on race, or sex or ability status.

Anger   One of the first reactions many staff feel is anger: anger at having their mind-set so radically challenged on so many highly emotionally and politically charged subjects, anger at having to make changes in all kinds of procedures and management structures when they already feel overloaded with tasks and committed to stretching performance targets.

If you are in charge of staff who are reacting this way to a requirement to getting their work, and their departments, into line with equal opportunities legislation, you need assertiveness to defuse their anger (see pp. 94–5), and to help them to focus on what needs doing. You may need to be clear, calm and assertive, using the absolutely basic techniques of core phrases, avoiding hooks, and so on, in order to assist them to stay with the fact that these things are now a legal requirement, whether anyone likes it or not. You can give assertive support to their efforts, and assertive positive feedback when they begin to get the appropriate changes in place. You can show lots of empathy without getting swamped by confusion and negativity. In fact, your assertiveness can be the positive framework you hold onto while managing a change such as implementing an equal opportunities policy.

DEALING ASSERTIVELY WITH NEGATIVE REACTIONS

Coping with your staff's anger

Coping with our own anger

You may experience anger too. You may also have a first reaction that the changes specified by equal opportunities policy are the last straw: that they increase your overload to an untenable degree, or that you are not in a part of your life where you want to put any energy into complex self-examination. You can use assertiveness to handle your own anger too.

First, you can validate your own feeling. All change-making, even when it is a change for the better, has a high stress cost to the individual. It is understandable to feel angry about being asked to cope with that stress. Allow yourself to accept your own reaction.

Look then at taking care of your own needs. This will enable you to work better. Share your anger with your speaking partner. Make sure you are fitting some explicitly physical activity into your work: anger produces a great deal of excess adrenalin, which is better used up in digging the garden or doing a sport than obliterated by alcohol or tranquillisers.

Prioritise clearly what you plan to do and then do not take the worry home with you (see pp. 112–3): that is, use your assertiveness to set a clear boundary on your obligations.

Once you have attended to your own anger in a positive and assertive way, you will find your energy is then free for you to direct it towards the actions you need to take.

Guilt   A second-wave difficult reaction to the implementation of equal opportunities policy is a sense of guilt. If a growing awareness shows up the fact that one has been behaving in a sexist or a racist way, or behaving in an ill-informed and patronising way towards people with disabilities, or making stereotyped assumptions about people with regard to their sexuality, one feels guilty. Guilt and shame are unpleasant feelings but they can, again, be assertively managed.

Assertiveness helps us to cope with guilt because it enables us to acknowledge a mistake without rolling in the dirt. The process is that of 'coping with criticism' (pp. 124–7), where, in this case, the criticiser is oneself. There is no need to feel defensive or to lose self-respect. The important thing is to acknowledge clearly that one has behaved in a way that one is not happy with and regrets it, but that in future action one's intention is to behave differently.

It can be useful to share this process with a speaking partner, in order to allow space for the emotion involved to be explored. It is important while going through a process of reviewing and revising behaviour to provide a balance to the upheaval of guilt.

The 'contact your strength' work (pp. 46–7) is highly pertinent.

The positive reaction to equal opportunities implementation improving within your organisation could be **excitement**. As a manager, you could have a real sense of how the resulting cultural changes would help develop the potential of your staff more fully, and raise the quality of your workforce. This can generate a good momentum within a team which you will be able to welcome and develop.

With regard to your own position, good equal opportunities practice might create an opportunity for you to re-examine your own potential. Use your assertiveness to become clearly aware of your worth and capability, and to apply for promotions without feeling inhibited by a stereotyped view of what roles you can and cannot fulfil.

Visualising and facilitating the growth of a culturally diverse organisation is indeed hard work for management, but it can be enriching and liberating too.

DEALING ASSERTIVELY WITH POSITIVE REACTIONS

Be aware of your worth

STANDING YOUR GROUND

You may feel that you are being treated in a sexist, racist or ablist way. If so, assertiveness is a positive asset in working out how to respond.

A formal complaint   If you want to make a formal complaint, get clear information about the grievance procedures in your organisation. Start to keep a record of the specific harassment or discrimination that you are suffering, with details of when and where it occurred and any specific effects it has had on your work. Also, keep a record of your own good work. Consult other women, or black people, or disabled people, or gay people in your organisation, to find out whether they are encountering the same behaviour. If they are, encourage them to keep similar records, but be aware that they will not necessarily want to support you or become involved with the complaint procedure.

When you feel ready to do so, consult your personnel officer about the grievance procedure and use clear core phrases and strong body language in all transactions regarding your complaint. Affirm your own good qualities often, and use your speaking partner as a resource for helping you to cope with the stress of going through such a procedure.

Complaining on the spot   Standing your ground may not be a matter of going through a formal grievance procedure. You may decide to deal with certain kinds of discrimination and

Gather evidence

Use assertive skills

Be prepared with core phrases

harassment by responding assertively immediately and in the context of the behaviour itself. This may mean working out core phrases to respond quickly to offensive slang words for women, for black people, for disabled people, or for gays. It may mean finding a strong and comfortable way of saying 'I don't find that funny' about sexist or racist jokes, or to find a clear and direct way of saying that someone is touching you in a way you do not want, or trying to engage you in types of conversations you do not want to be involved in. It may mean expressing the fact that you are unhappy working in an environment where sexist pin-ups are displayed. Any of these points could be usefully tackled on the spot and assertively.

No one should underestimate how undermining it is to be treated in a discriminatory way. After ten years in the assertiveness business I was astonished to find how shaken I felt recently by the sexist body language and attitude of a new male colleague telling me I had not done a task properly.

It took all my determination to stand my ground physically – he came right into my personal space and loomed over me like a real physical aggressor – let alone to prevent myself from gibbering inappropriate and excessive apologies. It then took some time and effort afterwards to think through how measured and grounded I had to be in both body language and spoken language with him until I had established a real base of personal power in my dealings with him.

Avoiding hooks   A senior administrator who wanted to say how she felt about sexist pin-ups in her office went through a whole series of 'not getting hooked' moves in order to make her point.

Formulate a core phrase

The core phrase she picked was

'I'm very sad to see those pictures there'

– since she felt that matched most closely her **feeling** and would be what she would most successfully be able to stay in touch with.

Stick with it

Two men in the office responded in a strangely orchestrated way, making alternate points:

'Well, I always say that women who object to that sort of picture are just jealous because they don't look like that themselves.'

to which she replied,

'I understand that you think that [playback] but I'm still sad to see those pictures there [core phrase].'

'Actually, that calendar was given to me by a woman.'
'I *can accept that the calendar was given to you by a woman [playback]*, *but I'm still sad to see those pictures there [core phrase].*'

'Nobody forces those girls to pose, you know. They do it of their own free will. If they enjoy showing their bodies off and I enjoy looking at them what's wrong with that?'
'I *understand you feel that way [playback]*, *but I'm still sad to see those pictures there [core phrase].*'

By this time she was feeling quite shaken and vulnerable but was delighted to hear the next answer which was,

'One or two other people have mentioned it actually, and I've been thinking about taking the pictures down.'

She then managed to remember the strong guideline after a difficult discussion, which is, once it is finished, *do not hang around*, and returned to her work. Shortly afterwards the pictures were removed.

Don't hang around

This woman recalls how pleased she was to find out how effective almost mechanically applied assertiveness can be on a controversial subject. She says:

'I could easily have got into a heated argument about any one of the points they raised, but all that would have happened is that I would have got upset, and they would have said – "There you are, hysterical woman, her opinion isn't worth anything." As it is, I did make my point.'

Ensuring support   Anyone who encounters regular discriminatory behaviour has a barrier to overcome in order to deal with it because that behaviour is eroding their self-esteem. Therefore, anyone who decides specifically and directly to challenge and object to discriminatory behaviour needs plenty of support. Your speaking partner may provide some; you may choose to be in touch with an agency or pressure group associated with your cause that would provide some – the crucial point is to make sure you have plenty.

The right to choose   Finally, remember that you have the right to choose **not** to be assertive. Pace your own energy. It may be quite impossible to take an assertive line on every racist comment, every sexist joke, every slur on disabled people or gays. Choose which battles you do want to fight and fight them, but also give yourself clear permission sometimes to let things go so that you do not wear yourself out.

INTERNATIONAL ASSERTIVENESS

Wider business contact throughout Europe, into the East and the USA brings UK management into contact with cultures all over the world. Assertiveness remains important but it needs fine-tuning to have the desired impact. The following comments are intended as thought-provoking pointers to the likely 'assertiveness quotient' in each country. They are indicative rather than definitive and based on the reflections of managers who have worked extensively in those countries.

FRANCE

Strong vertical hierarchies in many French companies and the power of the PDG (Président Directeur Général) may be a surprise to any manager who arrives from a flatter and more varied organisational culture. On a systemic level, the basic assertiveness technique learned and practised in Part I is useful in dealing with this comparative formality without feeling cowed. The informal relationships and discussions among company staff may be flexible, sceptical and energetic, but it is as well to be aware that in any public and recorded dealings formality and clear power-broking will be in evidence.

Meetings count as public occasions within this frame of reference. They are not a melting-pot for ideas and group process, but a forum for briefing, coordination and staking out of territories and power bases. You may find you need to be assertive in this context to a degree that would almost certainly be regarded as aggressive elsewhere.

It counts for a great deal to appear '*sérieux*' – that is, purposeful, professional and organised. So you may want to make a decision to adjust your personal style accordingly.

GERMANY

The shape of postwar capital financing in Germany has created an industrial profile of oligarchically run companies with paternalistic management cultures and long-term strategic planning fed by more or less continuous capital investment.

Assertiveness is crucial for the manager dealing with or working in the German corporate setting in a number of areas.

First, at a personal level (although of course this is consequent upon the social and economic ambience) the amount of privacy and personal space most people require is greater than in most other countries. The assertive manager must use empathy and sensitivity to arrive at a level of formality that feels comfortable and workable to German colleagues.

The deep permeation of German industry with long-term thinking, planning and financing generates highly methodical and rationalised corporate processes. It also fosters communications systems which are top-down and directive.

Criticism is rarely passed up the line as valuable feedback (except through the formal Betriebsrat or works council), but may be passed down the line freely on any failure to deal with work and communications methodically. The 'coping with criticism' mechanisms are therefore particularly useful. So is the work you have done on coping with your own anger, because the outburst of temper which might sometimes be tolerated in some workplaces as an understandable reaction to pressure and overload will, in Germany, be regarded as uncouth.

Respect for perfectionism in planning and execution and what it can achieve is balanced by a dislike for behaviour that might be praised elsewhere: taking initiatives, being opportunistic and making imaginative leaps are not considered alternatives to proper research and steady consideration. This may, again, mean that visiting managers need to take an assertive decision to adapt their reactive behaviour in order to be more effective in Germany.

ITALY

Flexibility is the key to successful management in Italy, where even the largest companies have a familial feel in the matter of power and lines of command. While there may be a clear reporting line in lower and middle management, managers working in Italy notice that in the upper levels it is through personal alliances that decisions get made and things get done. Because success in this sort of environment depends a great deal on personal qualities, senior management in Italy are very interested in what makes a good leader. They value charisma, empathy and an impressive but attractive aura. You need to contact your strength and find as much personal confidence and style as you can to work well in this arena, and your antennae need to work well to monitor the subtext in meetings you attend.

Meetings may be fluent, interesting and discursive, but people who have worked long in Italy often feel that decisions reached in meetings are less important than decisions reached away from them. An assertive visiting manager, then, will probably want to manage their energies by realising they need to prioritise the development of involvement and alliances with colleagues rather than investing heavily in crisp or bravura performances at meetings.

The giving and taking of clear criticisms and open file appraisal systems are not widespread in Italy, so exchange of feedback in that sense may not be appropriate. However, you can be assertively frank about any errors you make, as there is a high tolerance for genuine mistakes so long as any apology is equally genuine.

There is, on the other hand, a very low tolerance of arrogance or anything that could be mistaken for it. Self-esteem and self-promotion have to be done gracefully to be acceptable in Italy, so assertive communication would work better at the mellifluous rather than the brusque end of the spectrum.

THE NETHERLANDS

The Netherlands is a very open economy with 60 per cent imports and 60 per cent exports. It has an industrial atmosphere which manages to be both innovative *and* conservative. Organisations are lean and practical and the bottom-line is the paramount consideration. Hierarchies are shallow and the boundaries between roles are flexible – the boss is regarded as the most important collaborator in the team and strategy is communicated clearly right down the line.

Assertiveness is essential for the manager working with or within the Netherlands, both in self-management and in interactive work. Assertive self-management is essential for control of work because lateness, missed appointments, postponements and late delivery to a Dutch colleague will signal untrustworthiness and will quickly undermine your working relationship.

Assertive interactive behaviour is useful because, although collaboration is seen as the prime skill, meetings have a robust atmosphere. The exchange of views which leads to the final decision is often very blunt. Use core phrases and cut out padding to fit in well to this context. Also check your body language and face for the relaxed/alert state if you are receiving comment which is more blunt than that to which you are accustomed. In a highly collaborative culture an idea is not necessarily as closely identified with its owner as in a culture where individual originality ranks higher than teamwork: so points raised against suggestions you make need not be taken personally.

As well as receiving blunt comment well, your own contributions will be more effective if you frame them directly and assertively. Self-deprecation, a necessary courtesy in some cultures, is seen as pretension here, so a style which is not aggressive but is firm and forthright is a great asset.

The Spanish economy expanded rapidly during the 1980s and the stock exchange was restructured, providing alternatives to the bank financing which was the only source of capital investment previously. The expansion triggered a skills shortage and a shortage of managerial personnel.

SPAIN

There tends to be a generation gap in Spanish management between those over 50, who gained their corporate experience in the traditional Spanish corporate culture, and younger managers, many of whom have trained abroad in management theory and systems and are starting to function in a different way.

A strong vertical personal hierarchy is still highly characteristic in Spanish companies, with closed-door management and little in the way of paper communication through the organisation. A credible leader needs to be seen as a benevolent autocrat: sharing decision-making with subordinates may be seen as weak, so it is important to establish yourself as a firm and decisive character before attempting to work in a participative way. Use positive assertiveness – clear body language and good voice quality, with unpadded core phrases – to help yourself to fulfil this role.

A high sense of ownership of ideas is normal, and because formal job and role definition is rare in Spanish companies it is essential to develop a credible and energetic way of giving instructions: most delegation is simply passing specific instructions down the line.

An atmosphere of recurrent crisis may prevail because of a dislike of organisational systems, and an ability to cope is seen as a strength. You can use your knowledge of assertiveness to recognise a panic culture when you see it, but not necessarily to participate in or validate the panic itself. It is another aspect of 'not getting hooked' to be able to avoid getting sucked into cultural modes you do not like.

Formal appraisal systems are rare. Top–down criticism is accepted without any protest because it is seen as a natural part of hierarchical behaviour, so if you are in a supervisory position you can give critical feedback fairly directly. But criticism or critical points you want to make to peers must be handled much more diplomatically.

Energy is well used in developing a strong identity within the organisation and strong affiliations with colleagues. Although personal strength and authority are admired, abrasive egotism is not, so the power-within model of assertive confidence is ideal.

BELGIUM

About 5.5 million of the 10 million population of Belgium live in the northern part of the country, Flanders, and speak Flemish, a language close to Dutch; 3.5 million Walloons live in the South and speak French. The remaining 1 million live in Brussels, increasingly a political and multinational corporate nexus, which is predominantly French-speaking. People tend to identify themselves as Walloons or Flemings first, Europeans second and Belgians third, so there is a much weaker sense of national identity than outsiders might assume.

There is a low-key and relaxed atmosphere in the corporate cultures of both Flanders and Wallonia, where high-key and up-front assertiveness would be out of place. The real strength of assertiveness applied here is the emphasis on constructive compromise – on steady effort and work from all quarters towards win–win solutions.

DENMARK

Denmark has a small, highly developed and specialised economy. A workforce of about two million is spread among 6000 companies, more than half of which have fewer than 200 employees.

The hierarchy in most Danish organisations is chiefly functional rather than chiefly status-orientated, and there is plenty of communication and exchange of information throughout the structure. When there is a problem the priority is not to cover up or to assign blame, but to have an open discussion and form strategies to prevent a repeated mistake. Your assertive skill in acknowledging mistakes without rolling in the dirt will enable you to mesh in with this constructive behaviour in a good way.

The same openness is apparent in meetings, where, even though there may not be complete consensus, it is considered very important for all participants to have full information on all issues.

The type of leadership welcomed and well engaged with in Denmark is team leadership where the leader nurtures the team and leads by strong example of professionalism and confidence. So any tendency towards the aggressive mode must be moderated, and the quality of one's work has to speak for one without any other overt self-advertisement.

GREECE

Greece has an industrial core of large conglomerates run by dynastic families and closely associated with the banks. Next are the many small family-owned companies which have survived by learning to be opportunistic and flexible to remain viable through regular social, political and economic upheavals. Foreign investment has been focused on the tourist industry, which brings over 8 million visitors to Greece each year.

A powerful boss in charge of a narrow vertical hierarchy of subordinates is the norm: tasks, not responsibility, are delegated. Planning documents are more negotiation aids with financial sources than anything else.

Meetings are lively and characterised by energetic argument. If unanimity or consensus cannot be reached, the meeting will be reconvened. The two most important points for the visiting manager to be aware of with regard to assertiveness are that personal qualities of charisma and trustworthiness are rated higher than qualifications or competence, and that passionate debate is, for Greeks, a rather relaxing and companionable way of spending time. The first of these points means that it is important to prioritise developing personal relationships and affiliations with members of the organisation with whom you are working or dealing. Use your assertiveness to be friendly and confident. Shyness on your part may be read as stand-offishness, and you need to prepare assertively evasive answers to the probing personal questions you may well be asked – there is far less behind the privacy barrier in Greek discourse than in many others.

The second point is to notice that to take part in a heated debate is not, in Greece, felt to be aggressive or out of the ordinary – eloquence and expressiveness are much enjoyed. Use your assertiveness to avoid being steam-rollered and to join in equally energetically yourself.

When you are shouting at each other, things are going healthily and well. A colleague going silent during an exchange of views is much more of a cause for alarm. Do some assertive prompting so that they do not take a heavy sense of resentment or grievance away with them.

PORTUGAL

The revolution of 1974 changed many aspects of Portuguese social and political life but left the civil service more or less intact. The large state-owned companies which now exist are compartmentalised and bureaucratic, whereas smaller family-owned concerns are more unstructured.

Leadership is top-down and the line of command is based on personal loyalties rather than management systems; most procedures are variable and negotiable and clear job descriptions are a rarity. Assertive use of personal contacts and affiliations is once again important.

Meetings are for briefing and discussion and are not expected to arrive at conclusions or action plans. Although a relaxed and easy-going tone may prevail unofficially between colleagues, meetings are used for competitive power-broking, so you must be prepared to take your own level of assertiveness up a few gears. You may also want to use assertive communications to close deals and emphasise deadlines, delivery dates, etc.

THE USA

The USA is enormous and behaviour within its vast business world correspondingly diverse. The points made here refer particularly to issues which do sometimes give rise to misapprehensions and misunderstandings.

Much of the management theory studied, absorbed and implemented in Europe and the UK in the 1970s and 1980s originated in America, in the twin key concepts of systems and control. Job functions are well defined, lines of accountability and reporting are clear, and all processes are regularly quantitatively analysed. The needs of the individual are subsidiary to the needs of an organisation, and personnel are hired and fired according to whether they fit a needed job function at that time or not. Staff retain somewhat of a detached attitude to their employers for that reason, while taking it as read that, while they **are** on the payroll, their loyalty to the company and its products will be intense. It could be said that their loyalty is pragmatic rather than personal.

Social standing is gained by an individual who works for a prestigious company, but, if the company's fortunes flounder, that social prestige does too.

'Aggression' is a positive word, meaning vigorous pursuit of personal and corporate goals. Visiting managers from cultures where obvious dynamism is not valued will have to adapt to an uninhibitedly assertive approach to all behaviour in the workplace.

Authoritative and exhortative behaviour is seen as good leadership, along the lines of the involved and highly visible coaches in American sports. Meetings are chiefly for briefing and presentations and do not expect to make decisions or action plans. The decisions have already been made and the action plans are what is being presented. This is quite different from the collaborative 'kicking ideas around' model of meetings prevalent in more collaborative settings.

Because of the emphasis on and investment in checking performance and processes there is a general dislike for unsubstantiated theory, and irritation with any consultation which is not clearly thought through in advance, including the amassing of all necessary data. Good self-management and work control are important if the visiting manager is not to feel and be perceived as woolly and confused.

Although there is a superficial informality in the immediate adoption of first names and lack of elaborate social ritual, there is underneath a clear code of manners to which it is important to be sensitive. Empathy, sensitivity and active listening all help in raising one's own awareness and in interacting well.

JAPAN

Japanese investment in operations throughout Europe has brought Japanese management culture, peripherally at least, into everybody's lives. The enormous success of Japanese companies fills other recession-hit businesses with envy and Japanese methods are now studied with anxious attention from all sides.

These methods arise from the scientific management techniques developed in the USA with other factors added in: craftsmanship, perfectionism, corporate pride, excellent teamworking. These values and methods will not work in a confrontational or a directive culture, but they work superlatively in a team-based one.

Leadership is focused on getting the group to work together, and for non-Japanese managers the first conceptual hurdle to get over is that in this context the needs of the group really are understood to supersede the needs of the individual. This is not the case in business culture anywhere else, where, in the last analysis, the needs of the individual **are** seen as more important.

This profound commitment to and involvement in the group means that ideas are group-owned to a depth that would be unimaginable anywhere else. If you are about to become involved with a Japanese company, part of your assertive preparation should certainly be to take this clearly on board.

Communications between Japanese and Europeans are notoriously difficult both ways, because language, body language, manners and even the use of empathy and listening are confusingly different. The polite evasions, elliptical statements and indecisiveness used by the Japanese to avoid anything like confrontation, which they would find embarrassing, are irritating and bewildering to European colleagues. The European habit of reassurance and immediate congratulations on a job well done is offensive to a Japanese subordinate, because it suggests their good performance was not a foregone conclusion. Despite intense loyalty, inter-group competition and factionalism are rife, and the visiting or consulting manager from outside needs to have his or her antennae working well to read what is going on.

The overriding concern to preserve calm and courtesy means that any emotional outbursts are considered disruptive and a sign of weakness. Consequently an assertive control of emotions is necessary and you should make sure you have a trusted speaking partner with whom you can share any emotional overload that crops up because you are containing more than usual at work.

IN YOUR OWN BACK YARD

It is obvious to us that America is enormous and diverse and that several different kinds of atmospheres and cultures exist within the states. It is also obvious on reflection that all the countries we have talked about have a wide variety of regional and metropolitan subcultures, and good active listening and sensitivity are the first prerequisite in pitching your assertiveness at the most effective level for that particular environment.

It may be surprising and helpful to notice that as individuals we move in and out of several subcultures during the day without even leaving our own back yards.

The new generation of Black and Asian professional women report tricky crossover each day between the overtly assertive behaviour which is necessary at work and the personal style of behaviour which is acceptable in the family. Women and men in positions where a dynamic and overt leadership style is required say they find it difficult to ease up at home and may be more brisk than is appropriate with partners and children.

Look at the different ways you have to mediate your energies during the day, the different persona you have to draw on to perform in different job functions. For example, as a writer I have to be aware of managing the contrast between the 'high' which discussion planning and concept work engenders, and the quiet, calm, grounded state one needs to get into to do sustained writing. Essentially I have to be assertive with myself to work well. As a management trainer I find a very different form of control and monitoring is crucial – a relaxed/alert awareness of group process, and a pacing of my energies through what are often intense and concentrated days. It is also important to watch the energy levels on the days after a long or intense project is finished, since the calming-down process, if not managed well, can turn into inertia and inability to get on with the next piece of work.

Think about the different activities you have to undertake and the different groups, including those **away** from the workplace, in which you have to interact, and consider how your range of assertive techniques can best be used and modulated according to where you are, what you are trying to achieve, and who you are with.

10 Applied Assertiveness Workshop

*T*HIS step-by-step workshop takes you through some exercises in assertiveness to enable you to apply it effectively. Work on your own or with a partner, or use the material in some training sessions. Use the review chart at the end of the chapter to make notes.

STEP 1: POSITIVE VISIONING

Take 5 minutes to brainstorm (i.e. to write quickly, without self-censoring or inhibition) all the things you would like to achieve at work during the next two years. Review your list and circle every item which is either clearly realistically possible or means a great deal to you.

Now write a paragraph describing yourself doing all the circled items. Be positive and clear. Don't worry about how strange it feels – just do it. Notice what it is like to think of yourself and describe yourself in such a positive manner.

If you and your speaking partner do this exercise together, read your paragraphs out loud to each other. Speak slowly and deliberately, then take some time to discuss with each other what your reaction is to imagining and speaking about your future in this way. Does it make these aims seem more feasible? Is it a relief to acknowledge what your aims and ambitions really are? What other thoughts and feelings cross your mind as you reflect on these issues?

Now, continuing to take your intentions calmly and seriously, write for each item at least **one** action point, and next to each action point write a time target. If you are working with a speaking partner, share these with them too, and hear what theirs are. Give each other any feedback that feels useful.

This completes your positive visioning work. For the purposes of this exercise we have used a very open brief: what you want to achieve at work over the next two years. You can, however, use the same technique to explore any subject on which you need to do some positive visioning work. You will notice that it is a question not of indulging in fairytale fantasy, but rather of not getting blocked by negative feelings and unnecessary self-doubt. Whenever you need to form a positive vision, use the framework – imagination, selection and planning – to plug your energies into where they need to be.

STEP 2: BREAKING THE SPELL

This simple exercise starts to bring the myth and magic about refusals to the surface and to let it defuse. You can work with a partner, in which case have 4 minutes each (timed). You can work alone, in which case write your responses down during a 4 minute period. The exercise can be used in training sessions, so long as the group is confidential and an atmosphere of trust has been built up.

Complete these sentences, as many times as you can. Do not censor apparently irrational responses that come up.

(a)   'If I said "no", I would . . .'
(b)   'If I said "no", the person I said "no" to would . . .'

After the 4 minutes are up, change roles if you are working in a pair. At the end of their time, or at the end of your time if you are on your own, reflect on your responses, and notice what your internal reflexes are. It is not unusual to hear,

'If I said "no" I would be disliked by everyone.'

'If I said "no" I would be very isolated.'

'If I said "no" I would be thought of as "hard".'

'If I said "no" I would feel guilty.'

'If I said "no" the person I said "no" to would want to get their own back on me.'

'If I said "no" the person I said "no" to would be very upset.'

and even

'If I said "no" the person I said "no" to would die.'

By airing these reactions, you can begin to stop them preventing you from saying a good clear "no" when you want to.

STEP 3: SAYING 'NO' ASSERTIVELY

This is a role-play exercise which you could do with your speaking partner or in a training session.

1   A colleague under pressure wants to 'borrow' a junior from your department for a couple of days. You don't have any spare capacity either and you don't want to let him go. Say 'no' assertively.

2   A member of your staff is very keen to go on a training course but the dates are just when you expect a seasonal overload of work. Say 'no' assertively.

3   Your boss wants you to write next year's budgets over the next two days. You were not expecting to have to do this until the end of next month. You are really concerned that:

    (a)   doing it in a rush may lead to errors, and
    (b)   you are badly needed on current work in the next two days.

    Use your assertiveness to say 'no'.

4   A colleague has come to you very excited about a new initiative he wants to make. You can see several problems with it and do not think it can run. Tell him assertively that it cannot go ahead.

Take turns in taking on the role of the person who has to say 'no'. The other participant should try to hook you in every way they can think of. Be manipulative, be devious, be unfair, be emotional, be angry. Do everything you can to disturb your partner's equilibrium – this gives your partner the opportunity to practise standing by a refusal whatever pressure they come under.

When you are playing the role of the person saying 'no' be careful to make active choices about how much explanation you want to make, and how much, if any, regret you want to express.

After you have both had a couple of goes, share feedback on how it felt on both sides of the discussion.

STEP 4: CLEAR REFUSALS AND FUDGED REFUSALS

An anxiety felt by anyone working on the skill of strong assertive refusals is that they will hurt and upset the people around them. This exercise looks at what happens when you say an indirect and messy 'no', or a 'yes' when you should have said a 'no' and have to retrieve the situation by yet more messy explanations.

Use this as a framework for discussion with a partner or in a small group in a training session. If you are working alone write a short paragraph on each point instead.

1   Recall and describe a time recently when you said a clear 'no' to something or someone. How did it feel? What happened next?

2   Recall and describe a time when you knew you should say 'no' or wanted to say 'no', but fudged the issue and made only an indirect or partial refusal. How did it feel? What happened next?

3   Recall and describe a time recently when someone said a clear and direct 'no' to you. How did it feel? What happened next?

4   Recall and describe a time recently when someone said an indirect or partial 'no' to you, or a reluctant 'yes', when you can see in retrospect that they wanted to say 'no'. How did it feel? What happened next?

The learning point in this exercise is that, although a clear 'no' may produce short-term shock or hurt, the undeniable advantage of knowing where you stand means that things move on more positively thereafter. The aftermath of a fudged refusal, on the other hand, usually continues to be messy. Gradually building the skill of assertive refusal makes you a strong and easy person to deal with in the long term.

STEP 5: DISARMING ANGER

Try out some role plays where you are dealing with angry onslaughts from others. Use the following guidelines to help you.

In an angry situation you are trying to reduce the feelings of anger so that:

- you feel more comfortable

- you can begin to listen

- you can begin to try to **solve the problem together**

When someone is telling you off or is involved in a personal tirade against you, you can use assertiveness when you want to handle the problem rather than escape, or fight, or pretend there is not a problem, or simply try and calm the other person down (which would not solve the problem). You might use this whether the person concerned is a boss, a friend, a colleague, someone you live with, or some authority who is involved in a personal tirade against you for something you have done.

Suggested responses

(a)   Recognise the anger you are picking up:

'I can see you are very angry.'

(b)   Express your desire to solve the problem activity:

'I want to hear what you have to say. Let's try and work this out together.'

(c)   Get the angry person to lower his/her voice and sit down using a normal voice and a calming tone:

'Why don't we sit down and see it we can talk about what's happened?'

(d)   Use active listening to hear all the complaints before moving on to problem solving:

'It sounds as though this has been bothering you for a long time. This must have seemed like the last straw.'

It often helps to admit early on the possibility that you might have been part of the problem.

'Maybe I could have arrived earlier.'

'I want to hear what you have to say. Perhaps I made a mistake.'

This way of approaching anger assumes you are willing to handle the problem and move beyond active listening to try and resolve the problem. Simply placating the other person will only lead to further conflict and puts you in a passive role.

Role-play these examples:

1   You spilt your coffee over a colleague's computer keyboard. The machine won't work and she has a mountain of work to get through. She is furious!

2   A colleague feels you stole a march on him by meeting
    directly with a joint client. He is very angry, but you feel you
    acted reasonably.
3   You left the building late last night and locked up behind
    you. Unbeknown to you, another colleague was still inside. It
    took him an hour to contact the caretaker. His evening was
    ruined and he is irate.
4   You made a mistake which led a client into a legal problem.
    She is very angry.

As you can see, in some of these cases you are clearly 'in the
wrong', where in other cases it is more contentious. Deal with
the anger without either aggression or rolling in the dirt. If you
are acting the angry party, stay angry as long as you can.
Alternate roles with your partner, and, finally, share feedback
about what was easy, what was difficult, and how it all felt.

STEP 6: COPING WITH YOUR OWN WORST NIGHTMARE

Make a list of two or three interpersonal tasks which you
absolutely hated (in retrospect) or absolutely dread (in prospect)
as a manager in your workplace. These could include having to
refuse somebody's suggestion or request, having to confront a
sensitive personal problem, or having to deal with a redundancy
or anything else that makes you really tense. Be specific.

Working with your speaking partner, or in a confidential
group, choose the one which is your own worst nightmare and
work on that.

Briefly describe the background of the situation. With the
support of your partner or group, role-play the situation and try
out being assertive. Use the suggestions and feedback of the
people with you. Make sure, as part of the role play, that you
include meeting your own needs in the aftermath of the high-
tension encounter.

Take turns with your partner or other group members to focus
on your nightmare scenarios. Sharing resources about these
tense encounters is a good way to strengthen yourself for
dealing with them in the workplace.

STEP 7: BLOCKS TO POWER WITHIN

Use the following checklist, either in group discussion or making notes yourself, to identify anything which you feel blocks you from being in touch with your 'power within'. The checklist names all the basic assertive functions. Take time to notice anything which prevents you performing in this way. In any exercise like this, remember that to recognise is not to blame: identifying a block is the necessary first step to shifting it. If, as part of your discussion or writing, you can begin to see how to unblock yourself, then take time to reflect on this as well.

What might prevent you from:

- choosing for yourself

- having your own opinions and values

- speaking up for those opinions and values

- expressing your feelings

- refusing a request

- asking for what you want

- asking for help

- admitting ignorance

- asking for more information

- taking risks, e.g. trying out a new way of doing things, taking on a project, speaking out, having a go

STEP 8: FORCE FIELD ANALYSIS

Use the force field diagram on p. 157 to look at the factors militating for and against your ability to use your 'power within'. 'Power within' work is valuable because a solid sense of 'power within' is a key requisite for convincing leadership.

This simply structured diagram can also be used fruitfully to clarify any dilemma where there are 'points for' and 'points against', or any activity which feels blocked, or any developmental activity you want to undertake.

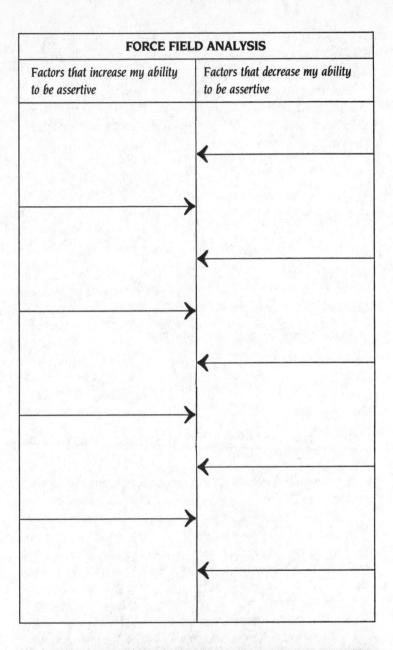

FORCE FIELD ANALYSIS	
Factors that increase my ability to be assertive	*Factors that decrease my ability to be assertive*

STEP 9: AGREEING AND DISAGREEING WITH CRITICISM

Do this exercise with a partner: either a friend or speaking partner, or within a training session.

Divide a sheet of paper into two columns. On the left-hand side write a list of adjectives or phrases which would be *justified* criticisms of you. On the right-hand side write a different list of adjectives or short phrases which are criticisms that could not be applied to you – i.e. are *unjustified* criticisms of you.

Exchange lists with your partner. Decide who will work on fielding criticism first. The other person then reads out the list they have received, *in random order*, as personal criticisms. Use the criticised person's name:

'Surinder, you worry too much.'

'Tom, you're very disorganised.'

'Maria, you're hard and uncaring.'

'Mark, you are a poor communicator.'

Move at random from the 'justified' to the 'unjustified' column.

The person receiving the criticism replies assertively in one of three ways. She or he says:

'Yes, I accept that. I do worry too much.'

or

'No, I don't agree with that. I'm not disorganised.'

or

'I'm surprised to hear you say that. I need some time to take it in and think about it.'

It is important, in the first two categories of reply, to say a definite 'yes' or 'no', to use an active verb like 'I agree' or 'I accept' or 'I disagree', and then to repeat the criticism more or less exactly. This makes your position clear in a powerful way.

You may be surprised to see the third category of reply ('give me more time') included as a possible answer in this exercise, but you will be astonished to find that, once you have surrendered your list to your partner, you may not be able to remember which criticisms were in the 'justified' and which in the 'unjustified' columns. You then have the perfect opportunity to practise saying, 'Hold on, I need to think about it.'

Once you have gone right through one person's list, change roles. Afterwards, share feedback on how it felt to say and to hear assertive responses to criticism.

As with all the basic techniques in Part I of this book it may feel mechanical at first, but it is effective; practise it and you will soon be able to use it in an increasingly fluent way.

APPLIED PERSONAL WORKSHOP REVIEW				
In this step	I was most surprised by	The most valuable point for me was	My action plan is	Any other notes
Step 1: Positive visioning				
Step 2: Breaking the spell				
Step 3: Saying 'no' assertively				
Step 4: Clear refusals and fudged refusals				
Step 5: Disarming anger				
Step 6: Coping with your own worst nightmare				
Step 7: Blocks to power within				
Step 8: Force field analysis				
Step 9: Agreeing and disagreeing with criticism				

Afterword

*T*HIS book will, I hope, have provided a clear description of assertiveness and guidelines for developing it yourself (Part I), as well as much food for thought about the various ways assertiveness may integrate well into your management skills (Part II).

Assertiveness will not always comprehensively prevent an explosion, or win an argument, or pull a team together, but it will almost always help to improve any situation, however tricky, and preserve your energies as you cope with the challenges you face at work. Its beauty is in its ability to make you a more proficient manager at the same time as enabling you to be more naturally 'yourself'. Once you have begun to use the methods and insights your assertiveness provides you with, you will wonder how you ever managed without it.

Further reading

Strategic thinking:
Negotiating: Everybody Wins, Vanessa Helps, BBC Books, 1992.
A Woman in Your Own Right, Ann Dickson, Quartet, 1982.
The Art of Strategy, Sun Tzu, trans. R. L. Wing, Aquarian Press, 1989.
The Tao of Leadership, John Heider, Wildwood House, 1986.
Mind Your Manners, John Mole, Nicholas Brealey Publishing, 1992.
In Search of Excellence, Tom Peters and Robert Waterman, Harper & Row.
Don't Ask The Price, Lord Sieff, Weidenfeld & Nicolson, 1986.

Stress management:
Stress Management, E.A. Charlesworth and R.G. Nathan, Corgi, 1986.
The Book of Stress Survival, Alex Kirsta, Unwin Hyman, 1986.

Physical well-being:
Are You Managing Your Health?, H. Beric Wright, Industrial Society Press, 1991.
Stretch and Relax, Maxine Tobias and Mary Stewart, Dorling Kindersley, 1985.
The Body Has its Reasons, Therese Bertherat, Cedar Press, 1988.
The Sensual Body, Lucy Lidell, Unwin Hyman, 1987.

Breathing technique:
Pranayama: The Yoga of Breathing, Andre van Lysbeth, Unwin Paperbacks, 1979.

Physical safety:

Her Wits about Her, Denise Caignon and Gail Groves, Women's Press, 1987.

Stand Your Ground, Kaleghl Quinn, Optima, 1983.

Self-Defence for Everyday, Paddy O'Brien, Sheldon Press, 1992.

Beating Aggression, Diana Lamplugh, Weidenfeld Paperback, 1988.

Sexual harassment:

Women and Harassment at Work, Nathalie Hadjifotiou, Pluto Press, 1983.

The Beauty Myth, Naomi Wolf, Chatto & Windus, 1990.

Racial harassment:

Racism and Recruitment, Richard Jenkins, Cambridge University Press, 1986.

Legal Control of Racial Discrimination, Lawrence Lustgarten, Macmillan, 1980.